East meets West

East meets West

Celebrity charity cookbook

Published by Accent Press Ltd – 2005
www.accentpress.co.uk

Recipes and articles © Individual contributors – 2005
Compilation © Accent Press – 2005

ISBN 1905170025

The publishers have made every effort to obtain the appropriate permissions from publishers and photographers. Please accept our apologies for any omissions, which we will be very pleased to rectify when East meets West is reprinted.

All rights reserved. No part of this book may be reproduced, stored in a retrieval system or transmitted in any form or by any means, electronic, electrostatic, magnetic tape, mechanical, photocopying, recording or otherwise, without the prior written permission of the publishers: Accent Press Ltd, PO Box 50, Pembroke Dock, Pembrokeshire SA72 6WY.

Designed, printed and bound in the UK by Butler and Tanner, Frome and London.

Contents

Preface

The Indian Ocean earthquake and tsunami of 26 December 2004 was an unprecedented, global, catastrophe, the largest natural disaster to which the United Nations has had to respond in 60 years.

It effected millions of people in 12 countries, spanning two continents and tens of thousands of visitors from forty nations around the world.

We will never know the exact magnitude of how many men, women and children perished on 26 December, but the figure is likely to exceed two hundred and twenty thousand.

Millions in Asia, Africa, and even in far away countries, are suffering unimaginable trauma and psychological wounds. Families have been torn apart. Whole communities have disappeared. Places of worship have been wiped out. People's anchors and values have been swept away.

The international community has come together in a response based not on our differences, but on what unites us. Opportunities are emerging to heal old wounds and long-running conflicts.

Under the leadership of the United Nations, we have seen a magnificent response – from North and South, East and West, governments and citizens, the media and the military, business and religious leaders, non-governmental organisations and international institutions. The British Government has so far committed £95 million.

Rebuilding shattered lives and communities and providing hope for the future will require sustained and massive assistance.

Two women from the West, but with strong ties to the East, understand this and have produced this book. They both met whilst living in Indonesia, where Barbara Jayson MBE was responsible for establishing the Foundation for Mother and Child Health; Jenny de Montfort was born in Sri Lanka and has kept up close ties with the island.

This compilation, with the support of many, is their contribution: all profits from the sale of this book will go to charities, UNICEF amongst them, helping with the long-term rehabilitation of victims of the tsunami.

I wish this book every success.

Emyr Jones Parry

Emyr Jones Parry
UK Permanent Representative to the United Nations

Introduction

East meets West is a collection of authentic traditional and inspirational fusion recipes with contributions from a variety of leading Asian and Western cooks, chefs, food and wine writers and selected embassies. Proceeds from the sale of the book will go to charities in Indonesia and Sri Lanka, the two countries most affected by the tsunami of 26 December 2004, and with which the producers of the book, Barbara Jayson and Jenny de Montfort, have close personal links.

Barbara and Jenny first met in Indonesia while on long-term assignments. Both became involved in charitable committees set up to allocate funds to various social welfare projects across the Indonesian archipelago. Recognising the inherent problems of child malnutrition coupled with the need for a charity vehicle to provide transparent and effective assistance, Barbara set up and ran the Foundation for Mother and Child Health; she was awarded an MBE for her work in Indonesia in the Queen's Birthday Honours list of 2004.

The Foundation's mission is to reduce malnutrition among young children through feeding and health programmes, pre-school education and small skills training for parents. The Foundation uses a holistic approach and strongly believes that only by linking and improving all these issues can any real progress be made.

When the terrible events of December 2004 occurred, Barbara decided she had to mobilise her skills and local knowledge of the area to help. It was evident that the large aid agencies were coping with the initial emergency. However, Barbara recognised that long-term rehabilitation was also critical and that its effectiveness depended on the accurate distribution of funds to the right projects. Her idea was to publish a book of recipes. As Jenny had experience of the wine and food trade in the UK, Barbara suggested they should team up to produce a book using a wide range of leading Asian and Western cooks and chefs.

The first person Barbara called was Nigella Lawson, and, though she does not know it, Nigella became the lynch pin of the whole project. Using her contacts in the wine trade Jenny got in touch with a number of leading wine writers and again the response was positive. In addition, photographers, agents, PAs and publishers all donated freely of their time, material and knowledge. In the end well over a hundred people from around the UK, France, Sri Lanka, Indonesia and Australia worked together to produce the book in record time.

In Indonesia, funds will go to UNICEF and the Foundation for Mother and Child Health, focusing on projects in Aceh and Sumatra associated with sustainable health, nutrition and livelihood programs.

In Sri Lanka, funds will be directed to the London Buddhist Vihara relief fund, START and the Navajeewana charity based in Colombo whose nominated project will be the rebuilding of Tangalle village in the south of the country.

Acknowledgements

We would like to take this opportunity to thank everyone who has helped put this book together. The goodwill has been overwhelming and the fact that over fifty cooks, restaurateurs, journalists and embassy personnel could respond so quickly was amazing. We were helped enormously by our contributors' PA's, agents, publishers, photographers and our friends whose cheerful responses have just made this a pleasure to put together. We would dearly love to name each and every individual but the list is too numerous. We thank you all.

We would particularly like to thank our brilliant husbands, Roger and Dan who encouraged us enormously throughout the whole project. We also owe so much to Hazel Cushion and Rachel Loosmore at Accent Press who have never been less than enthusiastic and have been unfailing in their support.

Finally we would like to thank the High Commissioner for New Zealand, The Right Honourable Jonathan Hunt ONZ for kindly hosting the book launch in The Penthouse Suite, New Zealand High Commission, London. Sileni Estates, Hawkes Bay generously supplied wine for the event.
Mark Thompson's Catering sponsored the delicious canapés.
For more information about Sileni Estates please visit www.sileni.co.nz
Mark Thompson can be contacted on 0208 540 9606 or
mj.thompson@blueyonder.co.uk

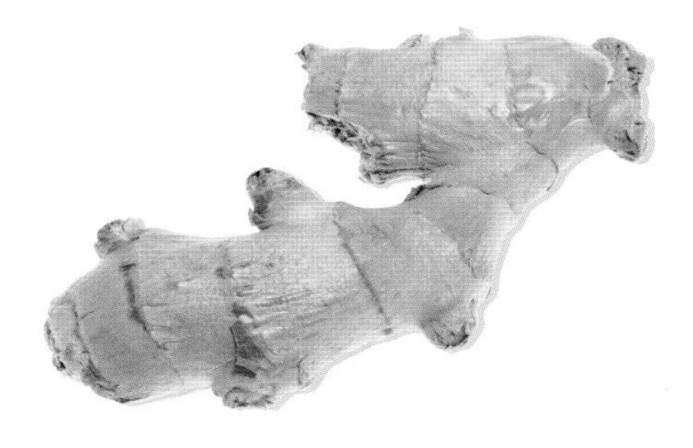

Conversion Charts

Oven Temperatures

Gas Mark	°C	description
1	140	very cool
2	150	cool
3	160	warm
4	180	moderate
5	190	fairly hot
6	200	fairly hot
7	210	hot
8	220	very hot
9	240	very hot

Weights

ounces	grams
1	25
2	50
3	75
4	110
5	150
6	175
7	200
8	225
9	250
10	275
11	315
12	350
13	365
14	400
15	425
16/1lb	450

Volumes

fluid ounces	millilitres
1	25
2	55
3	75
4	120
5	150
6	175
7	200
8	225
9	250
10	275
15	425
20/1pint	570
1¼ pints	725
1½ pints	850
1¾ pints	1 litre

BRUNCH

Keith Floyd

Keith Floyd needs no introduction; His television programmes and books combining cookery and travel together with his special brand of humour and knowledge have made him essential viewing and reading. Born in Somerset in 1943, Keith has now written 22 books, most best sellers and presented 19 *Floyd* series with an average audience of 4 million viewers per programme, TV series sales worldwide reach over 40 countries.

Lassis Yoghurt Drinks

Lassis are refreshing, sweet or savoury, cream drinks made from natural yoghurt.

SWEET LASSI

Serves 4

1 litre/1¾ pints natural yoghurt
100ml/4fl oz sugar syrup (see below)
6 ice cubes
some pomegranate seeds

To make Sweet Lassi, mix the yoghurt, sugar syrup and ice cubes in a blender until you have a frothy, creamy mixture. Tip it into glass and top with the pomegranate seeds.

LASSI MASALA

Crush together equal quantities of coriander seeds, peppercorns and cardamom seeds, enough to give you a heaped tablespoonful when they are crushed. Blend the yoghurt, as for Sweet Lassi, with 2 teaspoons salt and a quarter of the crushed spices. Tip into glasses and garnish each glass with the remainder of the crushed spices and some chopped fresh coriander leaves.

SALT LASSI

Make as for Sweet Lassi, but instead of sugar syrup, add 2 teaspoons of salt and omit the pomegranate seeds.

FRUIT LASSI

Purée any soft fruit of your choice, such as raspberries, strawberries, mangoes, apricots or banana, to make about 250ml/9fl oz and mix with 750ml/27fl oz yoghurt and 100ml/4fl oz sugar syrup and blend as before with some ice cubes

Courtesy of Harper Collins publication 2001

Peter Gordon

Peter Gordon is chef-proprietor of The Providores and Tapa Room restaurant on London's Marylebone High Street. Peter, often called the father of Fusion Cuisine in the UK, hails from New Zealand but did a formal apprenticeship in Australia before hitchhiking throughout South East Asia 1985-86 from where he draws much of his inspiration. Peter visited Sumatra, Burma (Myanmar) and Thailand and hopes that this book will bring some relief to the people of the region who have lost so much. Peter also is a consultant to New York's James Beard Award winning PUBLIC restaurant, to Changa restaurant in Istanbul and the newly opened 'Dine by Peter Gordon' in Auckland, New Zealand.

Melon and Kiwifruit Lassi

Quick and easy, and a great breakfast drink that contains all you'll need to start the day with a zing. Any variety of melon will work, although cantaloupe is my favourite.

Serves 2

300g melon, peeled and deseeded
2 kiwifruit, peeled and halved
200ml plain thick yoghurt
2–4 tbsp manuka honey
6 large ice cubes

Place all ingredients in a blender and whizz for 20 seconds. Add more honey if desired.

Taken from *A World in my Kitchen* published by Hodder Moa Beckett (NZ) 2003

Mango Coconut Porridge with Palm Sugar

This unusual porridge is creamy and moreish. The mango gives the sugar and coconut milk a fragrant fruity balance. For the best porridge, soak your oats in milk overnight.

Serves 4

200g (7oz) rolled oats
400ml (14fl oz) reduced-fat unsweetened coconut milk
40g (1½oz) palm sugar or brown sugar
1 mango

Place the oats in a bowl, add the milk and cover with clingfilm. Leave in the refrigerator overnight.

Place the oat mixture and 350ml (12fl oz) water in a pan. Add the sugar and slowly bring to the boil, stirring constantly. Reduce the heat, then simmer uncovered for about 5 minutes or until the mixture thickens.

Meanwhile, peel the mango and cut into thick slices, discarding the stone. Serve the coconut porridge topped with the sliced mango, or top with a little low-fat yogurt mixed with fresh vanilla.

Paul Gayler

Paul Gayler heads up the 40 strong team of chefs at the Lanesborough on Hyde Park in the heart of London. He describes his cuisine as "Global Contemporary", a careful blending of flavours, while retaining classic French techniques and values as a base, which he believes are imperative for any good cooking. His new book has just recently been published – *Flavours of the World* – a celebration of dishes using some of his favourite ingredients. Paul has also appeared on numerous radio and television programmes. He is married to Anita and has four children, they live in Essex.

Bill Granger

As one of Australia's leading food writers, Bill's first two cook books, *Bills Sydney Food* and *Bills Food*, quickly became international best sellers, and when the third, *Bills Open Kitchen*, was published in 2003 it went to the top of the non-fiction charts in Australia. Bill's books are now due to be launched by HarperCollins in the US in February 2005. Bill is a regular contributor to numerous publications in Australia and internationally. He has a regular column in Australia's *Delicious Magazine*, a food segment with Angela Catterns on ABC Radio 702 and is a regular contributor to the BBC's *Olive* and *Good Food* magazines in the UK.

Coconut Pancakes with Banana and Passion Fruit Syrup

Makes 18

215g (1 3/4 cups) plain (all-purpose) flour
1 tsp baking powder
1 tbsp caster (superfine) sugar
65g (3/4 cup) desiccated coconut
a pinch of salt
4 eggs, separated
250ml (1 cup) milk
250ml (1 cup) coconut milk
50g (1 3/4oz) unsalted butter, melted butter, for greasing the pan

to serve
6 bananas, sliced in half lengthways
passion fruit syrup (below)

Preheat the oven to 120°C (250°F/Gas Mark 1). Place the flour, baking powder, sugar, desiccated coconut and salt in a bowl and stir to combine. Place the egg yolks, milk and coconut milk into another bowl and whisk to combine. Add the milk mixture and butter to the dry ingredients and mix lightly with a metal spoon until just combined.

Place the egg whites in a clean, dry stainless steel bowl and whisk until stiff peaks form.

Using a large metal spoon, fold the egg whites through the batter in two batches.

Heat a large non-stick frying pan over a medium heat and brush a small portion of butter over the base. For each pancake, drop 3 tablespoons of batter into the pan. Avoid overcrowding the pan with pancakes. Cook for 2 minutes on one side, turn and cook for another minute. Transfer to a plate and keep warm in the oven while you make the remaining pancakes.

Serve the pancakes in stacks of three with the banana and passion fruit syrup.

Passion fruit syrup

115g (½ cup) caster (superfine) sugar
60g (¼ cup) passion fruit pulp

Combine the sugar, passion fruit pulp and 125ml (½ cup) water in a small saucepan over a medium heat and bring to the boil, skimming any scum from the surface. Reduce the heat to low and simmer for 10 minutes. Remove from the heat and set aside to cool.

Taken from *Bills Open Kitchen* published by Murdoch Books 2003

Photo: Petrina Tinslay

Darina Allen

Darina Allen is the owner of Ballymaloe Cookery School in Shanagarry, Co Cork, Ireland She works as a teacher, food writer, newspaper columnist, cookbook author and television presenter. She was also the founder of the first Farmers Markets in Ireland and is involved in helping set up new markets. Her passion for good food is emphasised by her role as Councillor for Ireland in the Slow Food Movement and President of East Cork Convivium of Slow Food. Her school is based on an organic farm and Darina is a Board Member of the Irish Organic Centre, Patron of Irish Seedsavers and a Trustee of the Soil Association in the UK.

Ballymaloe Strawberry Muesli

Best in Summer made with local strawberries in season.

Serves 8

4ozs (110g/1 cup) fresh strawberries
3 heaped tbsp (2 cups) rolled oatmeal (Quaker Oats)
6 tbsp (8 American tbsp/scant 2 cups) water
1 tsp honey

Soak the oatmeal in the water for 10 or 15 minutes. Meanwhile, mash the strawberries roughly with a fork and mix with the oatmeal. Sweeten to taste with honey, a scant teaspoon is usually enough but it depends on how sweet the strawberries are.

Serve with cream and soft brown sugar.

Taken from Darina Allen's *Ballymaloe Cookery Course* published by Kyle Cathie
www.cookingisfun.ie

Flaounes – Easter Cheese Cakes

Traditionally eaten at Easter to break the Lenten fast, Flaounes are prepared by almost all families in Cyprus. The cheese is made from a mixture of goats, sheep and cows milk and is similar to a fresh curd cheese, although rather firmer. A mixture of cheddar and Cypriot halloumi works well as a substitute. Flaounes are eaten at any time of day, warm at breakfast they are delicious and equally good with a glass of wine later in the day.

Yeast Dough
750g strong flour
1 sachet easy bake yeast
1 tsp salt
2 tsp sugar
2 tbsp olive oil
warm water to mix

Cheese Filling
225g cheddar cheese
100g Cypriot halloumi
1 tbsp flour
1 tsp baking powder
1 tbsp mint, chopped
1 tbsp ground hemp seeds (optional)
salt and pepper
4 eggs, lightly beaten

To finish
1 egg, beaten and sesame seeds

Mix the flour, yeast, salt and sugar in a large bowl. Add the oil and enough warm water to make a firm dough. Knead for at least 5 minutes until smooth and elastic. Put the dough in a plastic bag and leave to rise for an hour in a warm place.

Coarsely grate the cheeses, add the flour, baking powder and seasonings and enough beaten egg to make a stiffish paste.

Divide the dough into egg sized pieces and roll into 10cm discs. Place a tablespoon of filling on each dish and pull the dough up at 3 points to make a triangle. You should still be able to see the filling in the middle. Press the corners together and arrange on a baking tray.

Brush with beaten egg and sprinkle some sesame seeds over the finished flaounes. Bake in a hot oven 230°C for 12-15 minutes until golden.

Taken from *A Taste of Cyprus* published by Interworld Publications 1990

Gilli Davies

Gilli's passion for food spans thirty years from running a bistro in Oxford at the age of nineteen to writing and presenting a ten part TV series, Tastes of Wales, in 1990. Good ingredients, cooking and enthusiasm for exciting flavours motivate Gilli. Current projects include the publication of a *Celtic Cookbook*, establishing a cookery school in Yorkshire and a gourmet yacht charter in the Mediterranean.

Darina Allen

Ballymaloe Brown Yeast Bread

Makes 1 loaf

When making Ballymaloe brown yeast bread, remember that yeast is a living organism. In order to grow, it requires warmth, moisture and nourishment. The yeast feeds on the sugar and produces bubbles of carbon dioxide which causes the bread to rise. Heat (temp. 45°-50°C and over) will kill yeast. Have the ingredients and equipment at blood heat. White or brown sugar, honey golden syrup, treacle or molasses may be used. Each will give a slightly different flavour to the bread. At Ballymaloe we use treacle. The dough rises more rapidly with 85g (3oz) yeast than with 50g (2oz) yeast.
We use a stone ground wholemeal. Different flours produce breads of different textures and flavour. The amount of natural moisture in the flour varies according to atmospheric conditions. The quantity of water should be altered accordingly. The dough should be just too wet to knead - in fact it does not require kneading. The main ingredients - wholemeal flour, treacle and yeast are highly nutritious.

Note: Dried yeast may be used instead of baker's yeast. Follow the same method but use only half the weight as given for fresh yeast. Allow longer to rise. Fast acting yeast may also be used, follow the instructions on the packet.

450g (16oz) wholemeal flour OR 400g (14oz) wholemeal flour plus
50g (2oz) strong white flour
425ml (15fl oz) water at blood heat (mix yeast with 140ml (5fl oz) lukewarm water approx.)
1 tsp black treacle
1 tsp salt
25g (¾oz-1oz) fresh non GM yeast
sesame seed - optional

1 loaf tin 13x20cm (5x8 inch) approx.
sunflower oil

Preheat the oven to 230°C/450°F/Gas Mark 8.

Mix the flour with the salt. The ingredients should all be at room temperature. In a small bowl or Pyrex jug, mix the treacle with some of the water, 285ml (2pint) approx. for 4 loaves and 140ml (5floz) for 1 loaf and crumble in the yeast.

Sit the bowl for a few minutes in a warm place to allow the yeast to start to work. Grease the bread tins with sunflower oil. Meanwhile check to see if the yeast is rising. After about 4 or 5 minutes it will have a creamy and slightly frothy appearance on top.

When ready, stir and pour it, with all the remaining water, into the flour to make a loose-wet dough. The mixture should be too wet to knead. Put the mixture into the greased tins. Sprinkle the top of the loaves with sesame seeds if you like. Put the tins in a warm place somewhere close to the cooker or near a radiator perhaps. Cover the tins with a tea towel to prevent a skin from forming. Just as the head comes to the top of the tin, remove the tea towel and pop the loaves in the oven 230°C/450°F/Gas Mark 8 for 50-60 minutes or until they look nicely browned and sound hollow when tapped. They will rise a little further in the oven. This is called oven spring. If however the bread rises to the top of the tin before it goes into the oven it will continue to rise and flow over the edges.

We usually remove the loaves from the tins about 10 minutes before the end of cooking and put them back into the oven to crisp all round, but if you like a softer crust there's no need to do this.

Makes 4 large or 5 smaller loaves

1.8kg (4lb) wholemeal flour OR 1.5kg (3½lb) wholemeal flour plus
225g (½lb) strong white flour
1.6-1.7litre (2-3pints) approx. water at blood heat – use 285ml (½pint) of the lukewarm water to mix with the yeast
1 tbsp salt
2-3 well rounded tsp black treacle
50-100g (2-3oz) non GM yeast
sesame seeds (optional)

4 or 5 loaf tins 13x20cm (5x8 inch) approx.

Taken from Darina Allen's *Ballymaloe Cookery Course* published by Kyle Cathie
www.cookingisfun.ie

Gilli Davies

Glamorgan Sausages

These vegetarian sausages are a great favourite for a Welsh breakfast. The cheese used in the original recipe would have come from Glamorgan cows, a breed that has almost died out, but the cheese would have been similar to Caerphilly.

150g fresh white breadcrumbs
1 small leek, finely chopped
75g Caerphilly cheese, grated
1 tbsp fresh parsley, chopped
salt and pepper
pinch of dry mustard
2 whole eggs
1 extra egg yolk

Mix together the breadcrumbs, leek, cheese, parsley, seasonings and mustard.

Beat together two eggs and one yolk and use this to bind the mixture, adding a little milk if the mixture is still too dry to hold together.

Divide into twelve and roll into sausage shapes.

Chill in fridge for twenty minutes.

Fry gently in oil until crisp and golden brown on all sides.

Serve for breakfast with or without bacon and egg or as a snack later in the day with a fruity chutney.

Taken from *Flavours of Wales* published by Gomer Press 1995

Masala Baked Beans

This is an East-meets-West classic. I first enjoyed it at breakfast at the Tollygunge Club in Calcutta, and it is an Anglo-Indian treat that fills the gap at breakfast, lunch and anytime of the day.

Serves 1

1 tin of baked beans
1 red chilli, deseeded and chopped
1 red onion
fresh coriander roughly chopped

Prepare baked beans on toast the usual way. Just before serving, sprinkle with finely chopped red chillies, finely chopped red onion, and plenty of roughly chopped fresh coriander. Eat with an Indian beer or a cup of Assam tea.

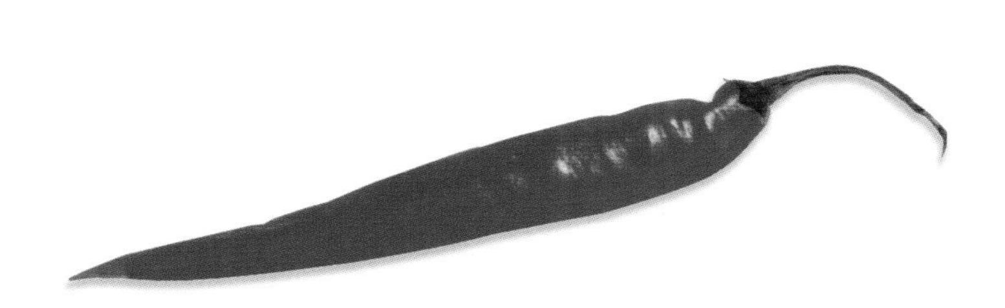

Sarah Jane Evans

Sarah Jane Evans is a wine and food writer and broadcaster. She is a past President of the Guild of Food Writers, a Trustee of the Andre Simon Memorial Fund, and a General Governor of the British Nutrition Foundation.

Photo: Juliet Piddington

Sweet Soy Mushrooms on Ciabatta Toast

Serves 2 • preparation 2-3 minutes • cooking 3-4 minutes

40g (1½oz) butter, plus a little extra for spreading
1 small garlic clove, finely chopped
350g (12oz) small chestnut or button mushrooms, wiped clean and halved
½ ciabatta loaf, sliced
2 tbsp sweet soy sauce
A small bunch of chives, garlic ones if possible, snipped into long lengths
Salt and freshly ground black pepper

Melt the butter in a large frying pan. Add the garlic and mushrooms and stir-fry them over a high heat for 2-3 minutes. Meanwhile, toast about 6 slices of the ciabatta bread.

Add the sweet soy sauce to the mushrooms and toss over a high heat for a few seconds more – it will caramelize instantly.

Put the toast onto warmed plates, and spread with a little butter if you wish. Spoon on the mushrooms and sprinkle with the chopped chives. Serve straight away.

Taken from *Ainsley Harriott's Friends and Family Cookbook*

Ainsley Harriott

One of the nation's all-time favourite television chefs, Ainsley Harriott has become a much-loved face on our screens, in addition to being the regular presenter of the hugely popular *Ready Steady Cook*, he has several other highly acclaimed television series to his name. He has sold over a million copies of his cookery books, which include *Ainsley's Barbecue Bible*, *Meals in Minutes*, *Big Cook Out* and *Low-fat Meals in Minutes*. Ainsley lives in London with his wife and children.

Alastair Hendy

Alastair was voted World Best Food Journalist and World Best Food Photographer at the 2003 World Food Media Awards. Seasonal local produce, and honest home food – whether British in origin or from far-flung shores, are all musts in Alastair's life. He is a contributor to the *Mail On Sunday* and was a hugely popular *Sunday Times* cookery writer. An inveterate traveller, Alastair spends much time eating, scribbling and photographing his way around the globe – and this is reflected in his cooking style. *Food From Our Travels: Asia* (publishers Mitchell Beazley) is his latest book. He is also the author of the Brit food classic *Home Cook* (publishers Headline).

Mushroom and Asparagus Brunch Rice with Poached Eggs

An excellent number for hoovering up leftover cooked rice, a wayward egg or two and any mushrooms or other veg that may be lurking – beans, mangetout, greens, that sort of thing. For quickness, use a ready-made bag of cooked rice, if you have no leftovers.

Groundnut or vegetable oil
1 bundle slim asparagus stems, trimmed
salt
3 shallots, finely sliced
4 cloves garlic, finely sliced
1 tbsp fish sauce
3 large mild red chillies, deseeded and chopped
1 tbsp sweet chilli sauce
1 tbsp dark soy sauce (or kecap manis)
200g shiitake or other mushrooms, sliced
250g long grain rice, cooked and cooled
1 small hot red chilli, very finely sliced
4 eggs

Heat 1 tbsp oil in a wok and stir fry the asparagus for about 30 seconds. Next chuck in the beansprouts and a dash of water and bubble up, so that the asparagus stems are cooked (al dente).Tip on to a warmed plate. Heat 2 more tablespoons of oil in the wok and fry most of the shallots (keeping some raw for serving) and the garlic until the shallots have frazzled at the edges, then add the fish sauce and chopped mild chilli and fry for a further 30 seconds. Add the sweet chilli sauce and soy sauce and splutter together for a further 30 seconds, to make a rich dark caramelised looking sauce. Next add mushrooms, the rice, and a drop more oil, and stir fry the mixture for about 3 minutes until it reaches a good deep colour. Meanwhile, poach (or fry) the eggs, keeping the yolks soft. Pile the rice in to 4 serving bowls, top with the veg and a soft poached egg. Scatter with the reserved shallot and sliced hot chilli – and put out the oyster sauce.

'I'm an eclectic cook. Asian and British my favourites - then I'll rifle through the Med or Morocco for more. But not in a hit-and-miss kind of way. Sometimes I'll be strict and stick to age-old traditions and cook things according to the way they should be done, for you can't go wrong with the classics. However, when it's a matter of what the fridge has on offer, then it's fusion time, and I make do with what I have. I've been branded a stylish cook - some refer to me as a chef, yet I'm self taught. Flavour always comes first.'

© Alastair Hendy 2005

Koki

Maldive Coconut Fritters

Pat Chapman

Serves 4 as a starter

The Maldives are a group of islands to the west and south of India. None is over two metres above sea level so the Tsunami caused them real damage. Years before, I took my honeymoon here, and my wife and I encountered kokis. They are a kind of savoury waffle requiring bespoke pretty moulds. These are dipped into the batter. If you have a waffle-mould use that. Otherwise just spoon dollops into the deep-fryer. Plain rice is satisfactory but any flavoured left over rice is even better.

125g rice flour
125g coconut milk powder
1 cupful cooked rice
1 egg
½ tsp turmeric
3 tbsp fresh lime juice
1-3 tsp chopped red chillies
1 tsp salt
vegetable oil for deep-frying

Simply mix everything in a bowl with just sufficient water to create a thick batter.

Pre-heat the oil in the deep-fryer to 190°C (chip-frying temperature).

If you have a waffle-mould, dip it ¾ way into the batter. Lower it into the hot oil. It should slip off into the oil.

Alternatively lower a spoonful of batter into the hot oil.

Add the remaining kokis a few seconds between each to keep the oil temperature stable. Deep-fry for about 8 minutes, serve with chutneys.

Nigella Lawson

Photo: James Merrell

Nigella Lawson is the author of five bestselling books – *How to Eat* ('the most valuable culinary guide published this decade', *Daily Telegraph*), *How to Be a Domestic Goddess* (British Book Award, 2001), *Nigella Bites* (WHSmith Award, 2002), *Forever Summer* ('as reliably mouthwatering as ever', *Time Out*), and most recently *Feast: Food That Celebrates Life* ('the kind of food you can dream of cooking', *Observer*) – which together with her successful TV programmes have made hers a household name around the world. She was *Vogue's* food writer for several years and is now a contributor to *The New York Times*.

Asian Spiced Kedgeree

Kedgeree started life, in India, as a dish of lentils and rice and then, translated into the kitchens of what could be called the Anglo-Indian Ascendancy, became an eggy, golden pile of rice punctuated with slabby chunks of smoked haddock. When I was a child it remained as a comforting brunch dish, still part of the homely repertoire of the normal British cook. Here, I've fiddled with it some more, replacing the earthier Indian flavours with the sharper ones of Thailand and South-east Asia and trading the strident tones of the smoked haddock for gentle, fleshy salmon, beautifully coral against the turmeric-stained gold of the rice.

Serves 6

500ml cold water for poaching the fish
2 lime leaves, torn into pieces
4 salmon fillets (approx 3cm thick), preferably organic, skinned (about 750g in total)
45g unsalted butter
1 tsp oil
1 onion, chopped finely
½ tsp ground coriander
½ tsp ground cumin
½ tsp turmeric
225g basmati rice
3 hard-boiled eggs, quartered
3 tbsp chopped coriander, plus more for sprinkling
Juice and zest of a lime plus more lime segments to serve
Fish sauce (nam pla) to taste

Preheat the oven to 220°C/Gas Mark 7. This is because the easiest way to poach the salmon for this is to do it in the oven. So: pour the water into a roasting dish, add the lime leaves and then the salmon. Cover the dish with foil, put in the oven and cook for about 15 minutes, by which time the salmon should be tender. Remove the dish from the oven and drain the liquid off into a jug. Keep the fish warm simply by replacing the foil on the dish.

Melt the butter in a wide, heavy saucepan that has a tight-fitting lid, and add the oil to stop the butter burning. Soften the onion in the pan and add the spices, then keep cooking till the onion is slightly translucent and suffused with the soft perfume of the spices. Add the rice and stir with a wooden spoon so that it's all well coated. There's not enough onion to give a heavy coating: just make sure the rice is fragrantly slicked.

Pour in the reserved liquid from the jug – about 500ml – and stir before covering with the lid and cooking gently for about 15 minutes. If your stove is vociferous you may need a heat-diffuser.

At the end of the cooking time, when the rice is tender and has lost all chalkiness, turn off the heat, remove the lid, cover the pan with a tea towel and then replace the lid. This will help absorb any extra moisture from the rice. It is also the best way to let the rice stand without getting claggy or cold, which is useful when you've got a few friends and a few dishes to keep your eye on.

Just before you want to eat, drain off any extra liquid that's collected in the dish with the salmon, then flake the fish with a fork. Add to it the rice, eggs, coriander, lime juice and a drop or two of fish sauce. Stir gently to mix – I use a couple of wooden paddles or spatulas – and taste to see if you want any more lime juice or fish sauce. Sprinkle over the juice from the two juiced halves of the lime and serve. I love it served just as it is in the roasting dish, but if you want to, and I often do (consistency is a requirement of a recipe but not a cook), decant into a large plate before you add the lime zest, then surround with lime segments and add the zest and a small handful of freshly chopped coriander.

This is one of those rare dishes that manages to be comforting and light at the same time. And – should you have leftovers, which I wouldn't bank on – it's heavenly eaten, as all leftovers demand to be, standing up, straight from the fridge.

Taken from *Nigella Bites* published by Chatto & Windus 2001

Rick Stein

Rick Stein OBE is one of the nation's favourite cookery writers. With his wife, Jill he owns The Seafood Restaurant in Padstow, which, every year, attracts thousands of fish lovers from Britain and abroad. They also run the highly acclaimed Padstow Seafood School. The television series that accompanied his book *Rick Stein's Seafood Lovers' Guide* won the Television Programme Award at the 2001 Glenfiddich Awards, while Rick himself in 2001 was awarded the overall prize, the Glenfiddich Trophy. His most recent fish cookbook, *Rick Stein's Complete Seafood*, has become the acknowledged reference book on the subject. Food Heroes, which accompanied the first series of the same name, was a major bestseller and his latest book, *Rick Stein's Guide to the Food Heroes of Britain*, is now available.

Nasi Goreng with Mackerel

The secret of a good nasi goreng is rice that has been cooked well so that the grains are separate, and which has been left to cool but not refrigerated. Leftover rice that has been stored in the fridge overnight does not taste as good. Like so many rice or noodle street dishes from South-east Asia, nasi goreng is a bit of a 'put whatever you like into it' sort of dish. However, it should always include a good curry paste, some thinly sliced omelette and plenty of crisp fried onion flakes. I always put prawns in my nasi goreng and I love broken-up well-flavoured fish like mackerel in it too.

Serves 4

225g (8oz) long grain rice
2 x 175-225g (6-8oz) mackerel, cleaned
2 large eggs
Sunflower oil for frying
6 large shallots, thinly sliced
175g (6oz) peeled cooked North Atlantic prawns
1 tbsp light soy sauce
5cm (2 inch) piece of cucumber, quartered lengthways and sliced
4 spring onions, chopped
Salt and freshly ground black pepper

For the nasi goreng paste

3 tbsp groundnut oil
4 large garlic cloves, roughly chopped
2 large shallots, roughly chopped
15g (½oz) roasted salted peanuts
6 red finger chillies, roughly chopped
1 tbsp tomato pureé
½ tsp blachan (dried shrimp paste)
1 tbsp ketjap manis (sweet soy sauce)

First make the nasi goreng paste: put the paste ingredients into a food processor and blend until smooth.

Cook the rice in boiling salted water for 15 minutes, until just tender. Drain. Rinse well and then spread it out on a tray and leave until cold.

Pre-heat the grill to high. Season the mackerel on both sides with salt and pepper. Lay them on a lightly oiled baking tray or the rack of a grill pan and grill for 4 minutes on each side. Leave them to cool and then flake the flesh into large pieces, discarding the bones.

Next, beat the eggs with salt and pepper then heat a little oil in a frying pan and make three omelettes. The object is to get them as thin as possible. Cook each one till the egg has lightly set on top, then flip over and cook a few seconds on the other side. Roll the omelettes up, leave to cool then thinly slice.

Pour 1cm (½ inch) of sunflower oil into a frying pan. Add the shallots and fry over a medium heat until crisp and golden brown. Lift them out with a slotted spoon and leave to drain on kitchen paper.

Spoon 2 tablespoons of the oil from frying the shallots into a large wok and get it smoking hot. Add 2 tablespoons of the nasi goreng paste and stir-fry for 2 minutes. Add the cooked rice and stir-fry over a high heat for another 2 minutes, until it has heated through. Add the prawns, the strips of omelette, the fried shallots and the flaked mackerel and stir-fry for another minute. Add the soy sauce, cucumber and most of the spring onions, toss together well and then spoon on to a large warmed plate. Sprinkle with the remaining spring onions and serve straight away.

Alternative fish

Try grilled and flaked sea trout, fresh sardines, red mullet, snapper or bream.

Taken from *Rick Stein's Seafood Odyssey* published 1999

Peter Gordon

Poached Egg on Crumbed Feta and Butternut

I ate something similar to this in Istanbul on my 39th birthday and it was fantastic. Try it with some blanched asparagus.

Serves 2

2 eggs
white vinegar
200g feta, sliced into 1cm thick pieces, pat dry on paper
1 tbsp flour
1 egg yolk, beaten
½ cup fresh breadcrumbs (try Japanese panko crumbs)
50g butter
100g peeled butternut squash, diced then steamed or roasted
2 tbsp extra virgin olive oil
¼ tsp dried chilli flakes
1 tsp chopped mixed herbs (coriander, oregano, sage, dill)

Poach eggs in water with a few tablespoons of white vinegar added. While they're cooking, toss the feta slices in flour then coat in the egg yolk and finally coat with the breadcrumbs. Heat up a medium sized pan, add most of the butter and fry the feta on both sides until golden and remove to two plates. Warm the butternut in the same pan in the remaining butter and place on the feta. Sit one poached egg on top of each pile of butternut. Warm the oil with the chilli flakes in a small pan then add the herbs and heat until sizzling then pour over egg.

Taken from *A World in my Kitchen* published by Hodder Moa Beckett (NZ) 2003

Potato and Bacon Rissole

Pat Chapman

This dish was my grandfather's favourite breakfast dish when he was serving in the British Raj in India. It is a great way to use up left over cooked potato at breakfast time. It is a breadcrumbed fried rissole, made of mashed potato at the centre of which is chopped ham and/or crispy bacon.

Serves 4

2 tbsp finely chopped ham
2 tbsp finely chopped crispy bacon
12 tbsp mashed potato
1 egg
2 tbsp golden breadcrumbs

Mix the ham and bacon, and divide it into four.

Divide the mashed potato into four, and, taking one of these quarters, carefully wrap it round the ham/bacon. Shape it so that it is a hockey puck shaped disc… a rissole.

Repeat with the other three.

Whisk the egg, put it into a saucer, and coat each rissole with it.

Dab each rissole in the breadcrumbs, achieving an even coating.

Heat the oil in a frying pan. Fry the rissoles until golden.

Notes

Notes

Pat Chapman

Pat Chapman was virtually weaned on spicy food, and, by the age of ten, he was learning from his ex-memsahib granny how to cook curries the pukka Indian way. In 1982 he founded the Curry Club to share information about recipes, restaurants and all things spice. Pat has written 34 books, with international sales topping 1.5 million copies. Many are on curry, but Pat also writes on Chinese, Thai, Middle Eastern, and all other spicy foods. Pat's business has taken him to many countries affected by the Tsunami.

I'm no different from any other exhausted tourist; given the chance, I enjoy lazy sun-worshipping on the safe-haven of an exotic sandy beach, dipping now and then into a benign warm sea to cool down. Like most other people, I had never heard the word 'Tsunami'.

On 26th December 2004 our innocence ended. Now we know that giant, high-speed waves are not the fiction of disaster movies; no seaside on earth is safe from them.

Since 1982, business and pleasure has taken me to the six countries worst affected by the Tsunami: the Maldives once, Sri Lanka five times, the Chenai area of India ten times, the Andamans once, southern Thailand three times, and eastern Indonesia once. How many times have I relaxed on those very same destroyed beaches?

I remember the smiling faces of hotel personnel, traders, hawkers, shop-keepers, taxi drivers and local inhabitants, kids and adult; friendly, helpful, wonderful people who can never do enough to please you.

I remember little things like the wizened old man in a white dhoti trying to sell me fake Raj coins on Chenai's Marina beach; or the skinny fishermen weaving their frail sailing-rafts between the razor-sharp rocks at Sri Lanka's Bentota to catch crabs; or the tiny Indonesian lass carrying a rusty tub teeming with tiny turtles in Sumatra's Padang town; or the school kids pestering for 'pens please' at Mahabalipuram temples, near Madras; or the crows lurking in coconut trees waiting to swoop down and swipe toast from unsuspecting beachside breakfasters at Sinclairs hotel located right on the Bay of Bengal at South Point, Port Blair, Andaman's capital; or two pet hens, much-loved Maldives island residents and the wild tropical fish at the same island enjoying being finger-fed on white bread; or the saffron-clad monk sleeping rough on the beach at India's southern-most tip, Kanyakumari; or the elderly women cooking Pad Thai noodles on charcoal braziers on Phuket's seafront.

What happened to them? I'll never know.

These recipes, my Tsunami 6, are dedicated to all those lost in the disaster.

But we can't bring them back.

More urgently, we must help rebuild the shattered lives of the survivors. We must all holiday on their beaches as soon as, and as often as, we can. Our very presence will send a strong signal that we are prepared to risk the Tsunami, and our 'dollars' will help provide the material support the region will require for decades.

Meanwhile, and in between visits, I commend you to enjoy the delicious tastes of the region with my Tsunami 6 recipes.

STARTERS

Mary Cadogan

As Food Director of top selling *Good Food* magazine, it is Mary's responsibility to ensure that all the recipes are great tasting, work perfectly and that the photography is stunning. Mary is very aware that most cooks these days have plenty of enthusiasm but very little time to cook. She believes that shopping well is half the story and is passionate about using food in season and making the most of British produce. Mary is an expert baker and making cakes, pastries and bread at home is her idea of relaxation. Mary is an experienced demonstrator and is a regular guest in the celebrity theatre at the *Good Food Show* in both London and Birmingham. Mary lives in Dorking, Surrey with her husband and two teenage sons.

Hot and Sour Coconut Soup

This is a really light subtle soup with plenty of fresh vibrant flavours. Adding the rice makes it more substantial for a main meal, though you can serve it without for a starter.

Serves 4 • cooking 25-30 mins

100g Thai fragrant rice
1.2 litres chicken or vegetable stock
1 stalk of lemon grass, thinly sliced
1 tbsp finely chopped ginger or galangal
4 fresh or freeze dried kaffir lime leaves, chopped or crumbled
2 red chillies, deseeded and finely chopped
250g boneless skinless chicken breast, thinly sliced
175g chestnut mushrooms, sliced
200g cherry tomatoes, halved
1 tbsp lime juice
2 tbsp fish sauce
200ml carton coconut cream
a handful of fresh coriander, roughly chopped

Cook the rice in boiling salted water for about 10 minutes, until tender. Drain and set aside.

Heat the stock in a large pan, add the lemon grass, galangal or ginger, lime leaves and chillies and simmer for 5 minutes. Add the chicken and mushrooms and simmer for a further 5 minutes. Stir in the tomatoes, lime juice, fish sauce and coconut cream and simmer for 5 minutes more. Scatter over the coriander and serve each bowlful with a little cooked rice spooned in.

This recipe first appeared in the September 2002 issue of *BBC Good Food magazine*

Mussels in Tomato and Curry Leaf Broth

In southern India the Tamils make a thin soup called rasam, which is usually served poured over rice. The British turned this into what became known as mulligatawny. Seafood rasam is a modern Indian adaptation and in this recipe we have used mussels. It's a wonderfully simple, quick and inexpensive dish, and can be prepared in advance right up to the point where you add the mussels.

Serves 4

2 tbsp vegetable or corn oil
4 garlic cloves, crushed
2.5cm/1 inch piece of fresh ginger, crushed
1 sprig of fresh curry leaves
12 tomatoes, cut in half
¼ tsp ground turmeric
¼ tsp red chilli powder
1½ tsp tamarind paste
800ml/27fl oz/3 cups fish stock (or water)
1 tsp black peppercorns
1 tsp cumin seeds
50g/2oz/¾ cup fresh coriander roots, washed
1 tsp salt
½ tsp sugar
400g/14oz fresh mussels

To garnish:
1 tomato, deseeded and cut into 5mm/¼ inch dice
1 tbsp chopped fresh coriander

For tempering:
1 tbsp vegetable or corn oil
¼ tsp mustard seeds
2 dried red chillies, split in half
10 fresh curry leaves
A small pinch of asafoetida (optional)

(see over for method)

Iqbal Wahhab

Iqbal Wahhab began his professional life as a journalist. He became editor of the *Asian Herald* and in 1991 he launched *Tandoori Magazine*. He then embarked upon creating his own vision of how Indian dining of the future would be and in March 2001 the Cinnamon Club was born.

Vivek Singh

Vivek Singh spurned family expectations to follow in his father's footsteps and become an engineer, he surprised them instead by announcing his intentions to be a chef. After graduating from catering college, he joined The Oberoi Hotel group as a specialist in Indian cuisine.

Heat the oil in a large saucepan, add the crushed garlic and ginger and sauté for 1 minute. Add the curry leaves and halved tomatoes and cook until the tomatoes are soft. Stir in the turmeric, chilli powder and tamarind and cook for 2 minutes. Pour in the stock and bring to a simmer. Meanwhile, coarsely crush the peppercorns and cumin seeds together in a pestle and mortar. Add them to the simmering stock with the coriander roots and cook for 20 minutes.

Strain the broth through a fine sieve into another pan, pressing down on the mixture to extract all the liquid. Stir in the salt and sugar.

Clean the mussels under cold running water, pulling out the beards and discarding any open mussels that don't close when tapped on the work surface. Bring the soup back to the boil, add the mussels, then cover and simmer for about 2 minutes, until they open. Remove from the heat and stir in the diced tomato and chopped coriander.

Now quickly temper the soup. Heat the oil in a small pan until very hot, then add the mustard seeds. They should crackle immediately. Add the red chillies next, followed by the curry leaves and the asafoetida, if using, then quickly plunge the mixture into the hot soup. Serve immediately.

© Absolute Press
This recipe is taken from *The Cinnamon Club Cookbook* by Iqbal Wahhab and Vivek Singh, published by Absolute Press.

Thai Fish Cakes with Dipping Sauce

500g/1lb 2oz fish fillets
half red pepper, chopped
2 red chillies, chopped
2 tbsp coriander
3 spring onions, finely chopped
2 cloves garlic, chopped
1 stalk lemon grass, tender part only, chopped
1 tbsp fish sauce
125ml/4fl oz coconut milk
1 whole egg
125g/4½oz string beans
vegetable oil

Cut the fish into small pieces. Place the pepper, chillies, coriander, spring onions, garlic, lemon grass and fish sauce into a food processor bowl and blend to a paste.

Add the fish pieces to the paste and blend well. Mix to a smooth paste with added coconut milk and egg.

Place the mixture in a bowl. Slice the beans finely into 3mm and stir into fish paste. Chill in a refrigerator overnight or for at least 2 hours.

Heat oil in the frying pan. Shape chilled paste into small patties with the help of a spoon. Fry in the oil until crisp and brown, turning once. Drain on the kitchen paper. Serve with Thai Dipping Sauce.

Thai Dipping Sauce

300ml/half a pint light soy sauce
2 tbsp sesame oil
1 tbsp honey
4 spring onions, diced
2 cloves garlic, finely chopped
2 chillies, finely shredded
2 tsp grated fresh ginger

Mix all the ingredients together.

Antony Worrall Thompson

He is passionate about organic farming and grows many herbs and vegetables for his restaurant. Despite such an energetic professional lifestyle, he still manages to find time for art, antiques, tennis and swimming (he swam the Channel when he was sixteen), gardening and of course his wife Jay and their two young children, plus two dogs called Trevor and Jess, two cats, twelve pigs and a variety of fish and chickens who all live at his country cottage retreat by the banks of the Thames. His latest books are the hugely popular, *Healthy Eating for Diabetes*, published by Kyle Cathie, and Little Books', *Well Fed, Well Bred, Well Hung: how to buy & cook real meat* and his frank autobiography *RAW*, published by Transworld, and the *Saturday Kitchen Cookbook*, published in May 2004.

James Martin

James Martin describes his cooking as 'Modern British with a hint of Mediterranean'. He has made a great impact since he began to appear on television in November 1996 and has rarely been off screen since, currently appearing on *Ready Steady Cook* for 8 years. His first book, *Eating In With James Martin* was published by Mitchell Beazley, October 1998 and his second *The Delicious Cookbook* was published autumn 2000 also by Mitchell Beazley, who published *Great British Dinners* in 2003 with a follow up *Easy British Dinners* which came out in March 2005.

Thai Prawn and Noodle Soup

Classic Thai soups often consist of clear broth poured into bowls, piled high with thin vermicelli noodles. This is a quick adaptation of a salmon and lobster soup that I occasionally make. Here, I've used fresh tiger prawns and added the shells to bought fresh fish stock to enrich its flavour and colour.

Serves 4

300g (10½oz) whole uncooked tiger prawns
1 tsp coriander seeds
2cm (¾ inch) piece fresh galangal or 1cm (½ inch) piece fresh root ginger, sliced
800ml (1pt 7fl oz) fresh fish stock (buy ready-made in a tub)
200g (7oz) thin rice or egg noodles (see ingredients notes)
3 tbsp Thai fish sauce
2 fat fresh chillies, deseeded and thinly sliced
2 – 4 garlic cloves (to taste) thinly sliced
1 salmon fillet, about 200g (7oz) skinned, and cut into small cubes
4 spring onions, chopped
1 tbsp chopped fresh coriander
1 tbsp chopped fresh mint
juice 1 or 2 limes
a little sesame oil (optional)
sea salt and freshly ground black pepper

Peel and de-spine the prawns, reserve the shells and set aside. Place the prawn shells, coriander seeds and galangal or ginger in a saucepan with the stock. Bring to the boil, then simmer gently for 5 minutes. Leave to stand for 10 minutes before straining. Return the strained stock to the pan.

Meanwhile, reconstitute the noodles according to the packet instructions. Drain and keep warm.

Bring the stock back to the boil and add the fish sauce, chillies and garlic. Reduce the heat and simmer for 2 minutes. Add the prawns to the pan with the salmon, and return to a simmer to cook gently for about 3 minutes, until both are firm and cooked. Add the onions, herbs and lemon or lime juice to taste.

Divide the noodles between soup bowls. Using a slotted spoon, lift out the prawns, fish and flavourings and place around the noodles. Season the hot stock and pour into bowls. Drizzle over a little sesame oil, if liked.

Ingredients notes
Galangal is available in most Asian stores – it is similar to fresh root ginger, but milder. You can also buy the noodles from Asian food stores, although many supermarkets now sell a good selection.

Zuppa de Pescatore

I first cooked this dish after being inspired by a picture I had seen in a cookbook a few years earlier. It looked fantastic and so appetising seeing a pan packed full of colour with all different kinds of seafood. I imagined the dish in the picture was exactly how local fishermen in small Mediterranean ports would eat it. I have since cooked it on a beach over a wood fire and even on a family sailing holiday (I had no fish stock so I made do with seawater and wild herbs). It was great sitting round diving into the pan and spooning out the fresh cooked fish and shellfish. It can be as simple as this to make a meal become part of your memories.

Any selection of fish and shellfish can be used – lobster, clams, mussels, chunks of skate, steaks of hake, gurnard and cod, the choice is yours; buy enough to fill the pan packed tightly in one layer.

Serves 4

1 shallot, finely chopped
2 cloves of garlic, chopped
olive oil
2 roasted tomatoes
Pinch of saffron
3 or 4 sprigs of thyme
splash of Pernod
selection of fish
570ml/1 pint fish stock
sea salt
parsley or basil, chopped, for sprinkling over the top
grilled bread
aioli

In a large pan, sweat the shallots and garlic in the olive oil. Add the tomatoes, saffron and thyme and stir together. Add the Pernod and tip the pan away from you allowing it to catch fire and burn off the alcohol. Add the fish and cover with the fish stock. Simmer for 8-10 minutes.

Remove the thyme and season. Finally, sprinkle with fresh chopped herbs and accompany with grilled bread topped with the rich, garlicky aioli.

© Absolute Press

Mitchell Tonks

Mitchell Tonks is co-founder and Executive Chef of the acclaimed FishWorks Seafood Cafés and Traditional Fishmongers. His various television appearances have included his own programme, *Fish Food*, as well as regular appearances on BBC2's *Saturday Kitchen*. He runs cookery schools from the FishWorks restaurants in Chiswick, Marylebone, Bath, Bristol and Christchurch.

Caroline Waldegrave

Caroline Waldegrave is co-owner and managing director of Leith's School of Food and Wine. She is also a cookery writer and health food expert. In June 2000, she was awarded the OBE in recognition of her services to the UK's catering industry. Caroline helps to write the Leith's Daily Recipe in the *Daily Mail*, and has done television and radio broadcasts, including a series on BBC2, *Tricks of the Trade* in 1994. She has appeared as a judge on *Masterchef*, and is a qualified wine instructor. She is a former member of the Health Education Authority (1983-1987) and a past chair of the Guild of Food Writers.

Spiced Butternut Squash Soup

1 onion, finely chopped
1 tbsp Thai green curry paste
2 medium sized butternut squash, peeled, seeded and cut into chunks
500ml/17½ fl oz good quality chicken stock
1 x 400ml/14fl oz can coconut milk
2 tbsp Thai basil, shredded
salt and freshly ground black pepper

For the garnish
Crème fraîche
Chopped fried pancetta

Sweat the onion slowly in the oil for 10 minutes.

Add the Thai curry paste and continue to cook over a low heat for 2 minutes.

Add the butternut squash, chicken stock and coconut milk, bring up to the boil, season with salt and pepper and simmer until the squash is soft. This may well take up to 20 minutes.

Remove from the heat and whiz in batches, and return to the rinsed out saucepan. Taste and season as required.

Reheat the soup and add the basil just before serving.

Pour into warmed soup bowls and serve with a spoonful of crème fraîche and the chopped pancetta.

Previously published in the *Daily Mail* 2004

French Onion Soup

This is a classic soup that seems to have come back into fashion. It is very important that the onions are cooked very slowly, as in the recipe, and are then browned as dark as possible without burning them. Choose a soup tureen that is not too large, the bread should rise right to the top of the tureen.

Serves 4 • preparation 10 minutes • cooking 1½ hours

55g/2oz butter
450g/1lb onions, sliced
½ clove of garlic, crushed
1 tsp plain flour
1.2 litres/2 pints good stock, preferably brown
salt and freshly ground black pepper
55g/2oz Gruyere cheese
1 tsp Dijon mustard
4 slices of French bread

Melt the butter in a large, heavy saucepan and slowly brown the onion: this should take at least 1 hour and the onions should become meltingly soft and greatly reduced in quantity. They must also be evenly brown all over and transparent. Add the garlic after 45 minutes.

Stir in the flour and cook for 1 minute or until golden brown.

Add the stock and stir until boiling. Season with salt and pepper and simmer for 20-30 minutes.

Preheat the oven to 200°C/400°F/Gas Mark 6.

Mix the Gruyere cheese with the mustard and pepper. Spread this on the bread slices and put them on the bottom of an earthenware tureen. Pour over the soup. The bread will rise to the top. Put the soup (uncovered) in the oven until well browned and bubbling.

Taken from *Leith's Cookery Bible* published by Bloomsbury 1991

Atul Kochhar

Atul started his cooking career at The Oberoi group of hotels in India. In June 1993 he graduated to the five star deluxe Oberoi Hotel in New Delhi. Here Atul worked as a sous chef in one of the five restaurants in the hotel, supervising a team of 18, raising the standards in the kitchen. In January 1994 Atul moved to the fine dining restaurant of Bernard Kunig, one of the best Hilton chefs. In November 1994, Atul moved to London to open Tamarind and in January 2001 he was awarded a Michelin star. In June 2002 Atul joined Marks and Spencer as consultant chef for their Indian range. Soon after joining, the Indian range was awarded seven Q awards in honour of its outstanding quality. Atul also teaches Indian cookery at Thames Valley University. Atul left Tamarind in August 2002 to set up his first Independent venture, Benares, which opened on 30th April 2003 where he also offers masterclasses.

Fofos

Goan fish rolls

Serves 4

500g Cooked flaked fish
1 Egg, white and yolk separated
1 Red onion, fine chopped
1 Boiled potato, grated
1 Green chilli, chopped
1 tbsp Ginger, chopped
1 tsp Toasted cumin seeds
1 tbsp Coriander leaves, chopped
1½ tbsp Corn flour
50ml Cooking liquor to moisten the mixture
Salt and Pepper for seasoning
Vegetable oil for deep frying

Combine all the ingredients together, except egg white and oil. Divide the mixture into 16 pieces and shape into croquettes or rolls.

Beat the egg white to stiff peaks, heat the oil to 180°C. Dip the rolls into egg white and fry in hot oil to light golden colour. Remove on to a kitchen paper towel.

Serve hot with spicy tomato chutney.

Langoustines in Their Pyjamas with Mango Sauce

Serves 4

20 raw langoustines or tiger prawns in their shells
20x12cm squares of filo pastry
50g unsalted butter, melted
10g pickled ginger (from specialist shop)
1 egg yolk, lightly beaten
vegetable oil, for frying
sea salt and freshly ground pepper

For the mango sauce:
1 large ripe mango
1 hard-boiled egg yolk
4 tbsp mayonnaise
2 tsp finely shredded basil leaves

First make the mango sauce: Peel the mango and cut off the flesh from the flat central stone; you should have about 100g flesh. Chop it coarsely, place in a food processor or blender with the hard-boiled egg yolk and mayonnaise, and whizz until smooth. Stir in the shredded basil, and season to taste with salt and pepper. Set the sauce aside.

Peel the langoustines or prawns, then make a shallow incision down their rounded backs, and remove the dark intestinal vein. Rinse the langoustines or prawns and pat dry with kitchen paper. Season with salt and pepper.

To dress the langoustines in their pyjamas: Lay a filo square on the work surface and brush it with melted butter. Set a ginger leaf in the centre and put a langoustine or prawn on top. Lightly beat the egg yolk and brush a little on the edges of the filo square. Fold opposite sides of the square over the langoustine. Press the long side to seal, then press the ends together to seal them. Wrap and seal the rest of the langoustines or prawns in the same way.

To cook the langoustines: Heat the vegetable oil to 165-175°C in a deep-fat fryer. When the oil is hot, add the langoustines in their pyjamas, 4 at a time. Fry for 3 minutes or until golden and crisp, turning them over a few times se that they brown evenly. Drain on kitchen paper.

To serve: Arrange the langoustines in pyjamas in the centre of the plates and garnish with the fried basil. Serve the mango sauce in a small bowl, on the side.

Anton Edelmann

Photo: Sodexho

After 21 years at The Savoy Hotel, Anton Edelmann joined leading catering and support services provider Sodexho in 2003 as the first principal chef for Directors Table, its fine dining division for business and industry clients in London. Anton is in charge of planning the menu and developing a signature menu range for city clients, training and motivating the team of chefs at Directors Table, running master classes for clients and staff, and developing and managing the fine-dining restaurant, Allium, in Dolphin Square, London. Last year the Anton Edelmann Culinary Academy at Allium was launched to develop and enhance the skills of Sodexho's chefs.

Josceline Dimbleby

Josceline Dimbleby has been one of Britain's most popular food writers for nearly 30 years. Her diplomatic childhood meant that she travelled widely and developed a taste for a wide range of cuisines at a young age. Josceline has published 16 cookery books and was cookery correspondent for the *Sunday Telegraph* newspaper for 15 years. Her cookery books have sold well over 2 million copies in the UK alone, and have been translated into many languages. She continues to travel widely, writes occasionally on travel and food for various publications, does live talks and contributes to television and radio programmes.

Eastern Fish Terrine

This fluffy exotic terrine, a first course fit for the most sophisticated dinner party (or lunch?), was inspired by a simple fish dish I ate on a boat trip in the remote and beautiful Andaman islands, which suffered badly from the recent Tsunami. Captain Beale, half Burmese and half English, was the owner of the small wooden boat, and his two boys caught and cooked the fish as we went along. Inexplicably I had to use that most English of fish, the Kipper, to reproduce the delicately spiced and smoky flavour I remembered. The terrine can be made well in advance.

Serves 6

225g/8oz kipper fillets
10 cardamom pods
5 cloves
1 tsp ground turmeric
½ tsp cayenne pepper
1 – 2 fresh chillies
2 cloves garlic
50g/2oz butter
juice of 1 lemon
1 tbsp tomato purée
2 rounded tsp gelatine
4 large eggs
425g/15oz plain yoghurt
fresh coriander leaves, to garnish
salt

Remove the skin from the kipper and chop the flesh finely. Put the whole cardamom pods and the cloves in a coffee grinder and grind finely. Sieve and then mix with the turmeric and cayenne.

Cut the chillies open lengthways under running water and discard the seeds and stems. Peel the garlic and chop finely with the chillies. Melt the butter gently in a pan, add the mixed spices and stir briefly. Add the chillies and garlic and stir for half a minute, then add the kipper, lemon juice and tomato puree. Cover the pan and cook over a very gentle heat for 10 minutes.

Sprinkle the gelatine into 4 tablespoons of barely simmering water and stir until dissolved. Add this liquid to the fish mixture and remove the pan from the heat. Separate the eggs, stirring the yolks into the fish mixture. Return the pan to a very low heat and stir constantly for 3 minutes, without allowing it to bubble. Remove from the heat. taste now, taking into account that it will be slightly diluted by the egg whites, and add salt only if necessary. Turn the mixture into a large bowl and leave to cool.

When the mixture is just cool and not yet setting, whisk the egg whites until they stand in soft peaks and, using a large metal spoon, fold them gently into the fish mixture a third at a time. Oil a loaf tin or a rectangular dish of about 600ml/1 pint capacity, turn the fish mixture into it and spread level. Chill thoroughly until set.

Shortly before serving, dip the tin in hot water and giving it a good shake, turn the terrine out on a board. Spread a thin layer of the yoghurt on to each serving plate, cut the terrine into thickish slices and lay them in the centre of the yoghurt. Arrange the coriander leaves around the edge of the terrine slices.

Taken From *Josceline Dimbleby's Complete Cookbook*, published by Harper Collins

Nigella Lawson

Photo: James Merrell

Thai Crumbled Beef in Lettuce Wraps

Given that I made this out of my head rather than out of a book, I don't know how authentically Thai it is, but I do know it's authentically wonderful. What I was after was that first course (among many) I always order in Thai restaurants, of crumbled meat, quite dry, sour-sharp with chilli, which you eat by scooping with crunchy, boat-shaped lettuce leaves.

One of the joys of this, in my version at any rate, is how easy and quick it is to make. If you're having people over to dinner midweek, you could make this as a first course before a plain roast chicken and provide a full-on dinner with next to no effort. Mind you, as a meal in its entirety, for three or four of you, it takes some beating, too. Reduce quantities (or not) for a five-minute supper for one.

You may need to be rather brutal with the lettuce as you tear the leaves off to provide the edible wrappers for the beef, which is why I specify one to two icebergs. If you want to perk the leaves up a little, making sure they curve into appropriate repositories for later, leave them in a sinkful of very cold water while you cook the minced beef, then make sure you drain them well before piling them up on their plate.

Serves 6

- 1 tsp vegetable oil
- 2 red bird'seye chillies, finely chopped
- 375g beef mince
- scant tbsp Thai fish sauce
- 4 spring onions, dark green bits removed, finely chopped
- zest and juice of 1 lime
- 3–4 tbsp chopped fresh coriander
- 1–2 iceberg lettuces

Put the oil in a non-stick frying pan on medium heat and when warm add the finely chopped chillies and cook for a couple of minutes, stirring occasionally. It's wiser not to leave the pan, as you don't want them to burn. Add the beef, turn up the heat and, breaking up the mince with a wooden spoon or fork, cook for 3 or 4 minutes till no trace of pink remains. Add the fish sauce and, still stirring, cook till the liquid's evaporated. Off the heat, stir in the spring onions, zest and juice of the lime and most of the coriander. Turn into a bowl, and sprinkle over the remaining coriander just before serving.

Arrange the iceberg lettuce leaves on another plate – they should sit one on top of another easily enough – and let people indulge in a little DIY at the table, filling cold crisp leaves with spoonfuls of sharp, spicy, hot, crumbled meat.

Taken from *Forever Summer* published by Chatto & Windus 2002

Aldo Zilli

Aldo Zilli is the founder and chef patron of one of London's most exciting restaurant groups which incorporates Zilli Café, Zilli Fish and Signor Zilli Restaurant & Bar. Great Italian food and Aldo's legendary sense of humour make these establishments a magnet for people from the media and entertainment world. Zilli Fish Too opened in February 2001 and won Best New Restaurant in the Restaurateurs Restaurant of the Year Awards 2001. The most recent addition, Zilli Café, launched in December 2001. Zilli has been actively involved in helping numerous charities. In September 2002 Aldo hosted a charity event in aid of Help a London Child which raised £50,000.

Tuna Coated in Black Pepper, Lemon and Virgin Olive Oil

A great dish for a starter or main course. If anyone in your party is not keen on fish served rare, place the fish under the grill once sliced for a few more minutes.

Serves 4 • preparation 10 minutes • cooking 5 minutes

350g/12oz fresh tuna fillet
30ml (2 tbsp) black peppercorns, crushed in a pestle and mortar
450g (1lb) rugola or rocket
50g (2oz) freshly grated Parmesan cheese
120ml (6 tbsp) olive oil
2 whole lemons
15ml (1 tbsp) sea salt flakes

Pre-heat the oven to 220°C, 425°F, Gas Mark 7. Roll the tuna in the peppercorns and place on small roasting tin. Roast for 5 minutes; the tuna should still be pink in the centre.

Meanwhile, arrange the rugola on a large serving plate. Thinly slice the tuna and arrange on rugola. Sprinkle over the fresh Parmesan cheese. Drizzle over the olive oil and lemon juice and finally the salt. Serve warm or cold.

Tofu, Carrot, Asparagus and Ginger Spring Roll

Peter Gordon

Tofu is a good source of vegetarian protein and it binds the other filling ingredients together in these delicious rolls.

Makes 8

1 medium onion, peeled and finely sliced
20ml sesame oil
8 shiitake mushrooms, stems removed and finely sliced
1 carrot, peeled and julienned or grated
1 thumb fresh ginger, peeled and finely grated
250g tofu, crumbled
4 asparagus spears, ends snapped off and discarded then finely sliced
8 x 25cm square spring roll wrappers
1 egg, beaten
vegetable oil for deep frying

Fry onion in sesame oil until coloured. Add the mushrooms and carrot. Fry until the carrots begin to soften. Remove from the heat and mix in the ginger, tofu and asparagus. Season with a little salt.

Separate the wrappers and lay them on top of each other in a diamond shape. Place one-eighth of the filling in the centre of the wrapper, going from the left to the right, leaving 4 cm on each side. Generously brush the point of the diamond furthest from you with the beaten egg, then fold the point closest to you over the filling.

Fold the two sides into the centre, then roll the spring roll tightly away from you, using egg wash to hold the seams together. Make remaining spring rolls the same way. Deep-fry in hot oil (180°C) until crispy, then drain on paper towels. Serve with chilli or peanut sauce.

Taken from *A World in my Kitchen* published by Hodder Moa Beckett (NZ) 2003.

Commendatore Antonio Carluccio

Antonio Carluccio grew up in north-west Italy. As a child he was initiated into the mysteries of mushroom and truffle hunting and his lifelong passion for fungi began. In 1975 he moved to London and became an independent Italian wine merchant. His hobby of studying and collecting wild mushrooms continued to flourish as he found wild mushrooms growing in the English countryside close to London, almost completely undiscovered.

He established his career in Britain as restaurateur, author and television personality. In September 1999 Antonio was awarded the Commendatore OMRI by the Ambassador of Italy. The equivalent of a British knighthood, the decoration recognises Antonio's knowledge, enthusiasm and life-time of service to the Italian food industry.

Stuffed Shiitake

This Japanese recipe also represents Chinese cooking because the shiitake mushroom, so popular now and available in every supermarket, is very commonly used in both countries (and indeed, increasingly, in the rest of the world). The recipe was suggested by my Japanese friend, Miho.

Serves 4

12 medium-sized fresh shiitake
A little plain flour
300g boned chicken meat, minced
150g shelled raw prawns, minced
3 spring onions, finely chopped
1 tsp very finely chopped root ginger
2 tbsp sakè (rice wine)
1 tbsp soy sauce
Olive oil
Salt to taste

Sauce
4 tbsp soy sauce
2 tbsp mirin (sweetened rice wine)
1 tbsp caster sugar
1 tbsp sakè (rice wine)

Clean the shiitake well and discard the stems.

Dust the inner part of the shiitake with the flour. Mix together the chicken, prawns, spring onion, ginger, sake, soy sauce and a pinch of salt. Use a little to fill the cavity of each mushroom. Fry the stuffed mushrooms gently for 5 minutes on each side in a little olive oil, covered. Uncover and add the ingredients for the sauce. Let them heat through and evaporate a little. Serve three mushrooms per person, with a little sauce on each one.

East-West Bruschetta

Commendatore
Antonio Carluccio

With great reluctance I accept the idea of 'fusing' ingredients from totally alien culinary cultures for the purposes of research. Very often these fusions are made for fashion or food snobbism, without complying to the rules of good taste and flavour. But here the combination of two totally different fungi, one from the East, the other from the West, makes for a light and simple, but sophisticated dish. I used the cheaper summer truffle to limit the cost, but if money is no object then you can use either Périgord or Alba truffles.

Serves 4

2 summer truffles of about 30g each
2 x 100g packets enoki mushrooms
4 slices good Italian bread for bruschetta
1 garlic clove
Juice of 1 lime
Extra virgin olive oil
1 tsp very finely chopped parsley
Salt and paper to taste

Clean the truffles very well and cut into thin slices, but not too thin. Cut the bases off the stalks of the enoki mushrooms.

Toast the bread until it is brown and crisp on both sides and rub very gently with the garlic. Brush with oil and divide between 4 plates.

In a bowl, mix the lime juice and 2 tablespoons of the olive oil with the parsley and some salt and pepper. Mix well with the mushrooms and divide between the slices of toast. Serve as a salad or first course.

Notes

Notes

Jane MacQuitty

Jane MacQuitty has been *The Times* wine correspondent since 1982. Her first experience in wine was as a small girl at her parents' table enjoying The Rank Organisation's cast-offs bought for a song, including first growth clarets, and Domaine de la Romanee-Conti burgundy. Her first job was with *House & Garden*, followed by a two-year stint editing the *Which? Wine Guide* for the Consumers' Association.

Cheat's Pimm's

An annual tried and trusted mixed summer drink with *The Times* readers is this Cheat's Pimm's recipe, my variation on the original and ever popular English gin sling. Ever since the producers of Pimm's No. 1 Cup reduced the alcoholic content of this classic summer sling, supposedly invented by James Pimm in 1840, to a measly 25 per cent and increased the price to almost £13 a bottle, I have done the decent thing and printed my Cheat's Pimm's version that delivers the correct alcoholic punch and flavour for a lot less money.

For every measure of good 40 per cent-plus gin, add a measure of red vermouth – French or Italian will do – plus half a measure of orange curacao. Give the mix a chance to mingle and marry for several hours and add a slice each per person of fresh orange, lemon and cucumber. I usually add a sliced strawberry or two, and a sprig each of mint and borage, if you have it, adds pleasing herby overtones. All you need do then is top up with ice-cold fizzy lemonade, or ginger beer if you prefer. One part Cheat's Pimm's mixture to four parts fizz is the happiest ratio.

SALADS

Antony Worrall Thompson

Chargrilled Thai Beef Salad

Serves 4 • preparation and cooking 40 minutes, plus marinating time.

1 tbsp jasmine rice, uncooked
2 dried red chillies
500g (1lb 2oz) thick fillet steak
2 tbsp sesame oil
75ml (2½ fl oz) kecap manis (sweet soy sauce)
2 tsp sugar
4 tbsp lime juice
3 tbsp Thai fish sauce
1 small cucumber, peeled, deseeded, halved lengthways and cut into 1cm slices.
4 red shallots, finely sliced
12 cherry tomatoes, halved
2 red chillies, finely sliced
1 handful fresh mint leaves
1 handful fresh coriander leaves
2 tablesoons fresh basil leaves, ripped
4 spring onions, finely sliced

Heat the frying pan, add the rice and toast until golden but not burnt. Grind the rice in a clean coffee-grinder or pound to a powder and set aside.

Reheat the frying pan and add the dried red chillies. Toast until they are smoky, then grind or pound to a powder and set aside.

Chargrill or pan-fry the beef for around 12 minutes, until well marked outside and rare to medium-rare inside. Place in a bowl and leave to rest for 10 minutes. Meanwhile, combine the sesame oil with the kecap manis and brush over the fillet. Marinate for 2 hours.

Dissolve the sugar in the lime juice and fish sauce. Combine half a teaspoon of the ground dried chilli powder with half a teaspoon of the ground rice and set aside. Combine the cucumber, shallots, cherry tomatoes, red chillies, herbs and spring onions in a large bowl. Add the lime juice and fish sauce mixture and toss to combine.

Slice the beef thinly. Toss the beef and ground rice mix through the salad with any cooking juices that have collected in the beef bowl. Pile high on a large platter and serve with a salad of crunchy raw lettuce.

Taken from *Antony Worrall Thompson's Top 100 Beef Recipes*, 2005.

Asian Steak, Mint and Cucumber Salad

Couldn't be simpler. Couldn't be tastier. And so slimming – well, almost.

4 good beef steaks - sirloin or rib eye, or use lamb steaks
4 tbsp bottled teryaki marinade (or soy sauce mixed with 1 tbsp caster sugar)
1 stick lemon grass, outer leaves discarded and very finely chopped
1 tbsp fish sauce
½ tbsp caster sugar
3 tbsp lime juice
1 tbsp vegetable oil
½ cucumber, sliced
2 long mild red chillies, deseeded and finely shredded lengthways
4 spring onions, shredded
1 small bunch each of coriander, mint and basil, leaves only

Toss the steaks with the teryaki marinade and the lemon grass, and leave on one side for as long as time will let you. Mix the fish sauce with the sugar and lime juice, then when ready to serve, toss with the cucumber, spring onions, chilli and herb leaves. To cook the steaks, remove them from their marinade, rub with a little oil, then sear them in a preheated heavy pan for about 2 minutes on each side, without moving them about. Serve with the salad piled on top or slice the steaks and serve the salad in bowls alongside.

© Alastair Hendy 2005
First appeared in *BBC Good Food* magazine

Alastair Hendy

James Martin

Seared Scallop and Coriander Salad with a Lime and Red Pepper Dressing

Basically there are two types of scallop – queens and kings – and there is a great difference between them. King scallops are larger than queens and are diver caught. They provide a much more substantial piece of meat, but at a price. Steer clear of queens which are small, and after cooking end up looking like buttons. And never – repeat never – buy scallops that have been frozen: when defrosted and cooked they lose all their flavour, leaving a pan full of defrosted water to boot.

10 large king scallops with corals, shelled
1 red pepper
Salt and freshly ground black pepper
Extra virgin oil
Juice and zest of 2 limes
2 x 15g (½oz) packets fresh coriander, half of it chopped.
1 tbsp red onion, chopped
250g (9oz) bag mixed salad leaves, pre-washed

Pre-heat the oven to 200°C/400°F/Gas Mark 6. Cut the pepper in half, remove the seeds and stalk, and place in an ovenproof dish. Season with salt and pepper, drizzle with olive oil and place in the oven for 15 minutes until the skin has browned. Remove from the oven and while hot, place in a bowl, quickly cover with clingfilm and leave to go cold. When cold, remove and discard the skin.

For the dressing, cut the pepper flesh into small dice and place in a bowl with the lime juice and zest. Add 6 tablespoons of the olive oil with the chopped coriander and onion. Season and leave to one side. Remove any black threads or sand from the scallops, but do not wash them. Heat a frying pan until very hot. Season the scallops with salt and pepper, place in the very hot pan and deep-fry on both sides for 30 seconds or until just cooked. Combine half the dressing with the salad leaves and remaining coriander leaves, and place in two bowls. Divide the scallops between two plates. Finish the dish by drizzling the remaining dressing over the scallops, and serve with the salad.

James's tip

Any salad leaves would do, but the pre-washed bags are handy. The Continental selections normally contain a blend of frisee, radicchio and lollo rosso, while the Italian one adds rocket and herbs.

Anton Edelmann

Photo: Sodexho

Baked Figs with Goat's Cheese and Coriander Salad

Serves 4

For the goat's cheese filling

2 small goat's cheeses (eg: crottin de chavignol)
a rosemary sprig
300ml olive oil
100ml double cream
6 black figs
finely grated zest of ½ orange
sea salt

For the coriander salad

2 carrots, peeled
2 spring onions
4 radishes
25g coriander leaves
50g wild rocket
juice of ½ lemon
50ml beetroot glaze, for garnish

To make the cheese filling: Put the cheeses and rosemary in the olive oil and leave for at least 3 hours or, better still, overnight. Take them out of the oil and pat dry with kitchen paper. Crumble them into a bowl and stir in the cream. Reserve the rosemary and olive oil.

To cook the figs: Heat the oven to 200°C. Cut the figs in half, sprinkle with a little sea salt and the orange zest, and top with the cheese filling. Place the rosemary on a baking tray and set the figs on the tray. Bake in the oven for 6 - 7 minutes until the cheese has melted and is lightly coloured.

Meanwhile, make the coriander salad: Cut the carrots, spring onions and radishes into very fine strips and mix them with the coriander leaves and rocket. It is essential that the rocket leaves are small and the julienne of carrots and radishes are very thin. Be sure to make the salad with equal quantities of every ingredient so that you can see each one.

To serve: Whisk the lemon juice with a little of the reserved olive oil and toss the salad in this dressing. Place 3 fig halves on each plate and top with the coriander salad. Pour the beetroot glaze over the figs.

Crunchy Thai Salad

1 tbsp jasmine rice, uncooked
2 dried red chillies
2 tsp sugar
4 tbsp lime juice
3 tbsp Thai fish sauce
1 small cucumber, peeled, deseeded, halved lengthways and cut into 1cm (½ inch) slices
4 red shallots, finely sliced
12 cherry tomatoes, halved
2 red chillies, finely sliced
1 handful fresh mint leaves
1 handful fresh coriander leaves
2 tbsp fresh basil leaves, ripped
4 spring onions, finely sliced

Heat a dry frying pan, add rice and toast until golden but not burnt. Grind the rice in a clean coffee-grinder or pound to a powder and set aside.

Reheat the frying pan and add the dried red chillies. Toast until they are smoky, then grind or pound to a powder and set aside.

Dissolve the sugar in the lime juice and fish sauce. Combine half a teaspoon of the ground dried chilli powder with half a teaspoon of the ground rice and set aside. Combine the cucumber, shallots, cherry tomatoes, red chillies, herbs and sping onions in a large bowl. Add the lime juice and fish sauce mixture and toss to combine.

Toss the ground rice mix throughout the salad.

Appeared in *Sunday Express Magazine* April 2005

Antony Worrall Thompson

Photo: Petrina Tinslay

Grapefruit and Prawn Salad

Bill Granger

2 ruby grapefruit or 2 grapefruit or
1 pomelo
40g (¼ cup) cashews
20 cooked prawns (shrimp), peeled and deveined
20g (1 cup) mint leaves
1 small butter lettuce, washed and dried
dressing (below)

To serve
steamed rice

Peel the grapefruit by slicing off both ends. Stand the end of the fruit on a board, and following the curves of the grapefruit, slice off all the peel with a sharp knife. Make sure the pith is also removed. Slice out segments of the grapefruit by cutting in between the membrane. Set aside. Place a frying pan over a high heat and when hot, add the cashews. Cook, stirring for 2 to 3 minutes, or until lightly roasted. Remove from the heat and roughly chop. Set aside.

Place the grapefruit, prawns and mint in a bowl. Add the dressing and toss to combine. Arrange the lettuce leaves on a large serving plate, or divide between four plates. Top with the salad and sprinkle with the roasted cashews. Serve with steamed rice. Serves 4.

Dressing
60ml (¼ cup) fish sauce
60ml (¼ cup) lime juice
2 tbsp brown sugar
3 red Asian shallots, or ½ red onion,
finely sliced
2 small red chillies, finely chopped

Place all the ingredients in a small bowl and stir until the sugar is dissolved.

Taken from *Bills Open Kitchen* published by Murdoch Books 2003

Wing Bean Salad with Mustard Seeds and Fresh Coconut

15 whole wing beans sliced (Chinese long beans or snow peas – mange tout)
1 whole red onion peeled and sliced
2 whole green chillies sliced with the seeds in
1 clove garlic sliced finely
5cm fresh turmeric root, peeled and sliced finely
12 curry leaves
1 tsp mustard seeds
4 tbsp coconut oil or vegetable oil
200ml coconut water or water
1 tsp curry powder
1 fresh coconut grated finely

Wash the wing beans and slice finely.

Heat the oil in a large heavy based frying pan and fry the onions and garlic until just browned.

Add the curry leaves, turmeric, mustard seeds and green chilli, fry for a few seconds.

Add the wing beans and curry powder and stir fry fast as to stop the spices from burning.

Add the water and salt and cook uncovered until the beans are tender.

Place on a serving platter and sprinkle with freshly grated coconut.

Fritz Zwahlen

Fritz Zwahlen was born on the outskirts of Berne, Switzerland's capital. He acquired a life-long interest in cooking from his Austrian born mother. Having trained in Switzerland he has pursued an international career before moving, with his family in 2004, to Galle, Sri Lanka. He now serves as Sri Lanka Executive Chef overseeing Amanresorts two new properties in southern Sri Lanka, Amangalla located within Galle Fort in the historic port of Galle and Amanwella, a contemporary beach resort located near the village of Tangalle.

Diana Henry

After a career as a television producer, Diana Henry started to write about food when her first child was born. She now has a weekly column in the *Sunday Telegraph* magazine and contributes to a wide range of other publications including *House and Garden*, *Red*, *Olive* and *BBC Good Food*, and broadcasts regularly on *Woman's Hour* on Radio 4. She is the author of two best selling cook books, *Crazy Water, Pickled Lemons* and *The Gastropub Cookbook*. She lives in London with her husband and children.

Thai-style Chicken and Mango Salad

To be strictly Thai you can leave out the watercress and increase the quantity of herbs. If you can't find green mangoes, or prefer to eat ripe ones, you can use 1 ripe mango and 1 tart green apple (core removed). As well as sourness the green mangoes provide crunch so an apple is a fine substitute.

Serves 4

4 chicken fillets (skinned)
salt and pepper
groundnut oil
6 spring onions, sliced
8 cloves garlic, peeled and finely sliced
2 medium-sized unripe mangoes
2 tbsp fish sauce
2 tbsp caster sugar
juice of 1½ limes
3 long red chillies
50g fresh coriander
40g fresh mint leaves
50g watercress leaves
1½ tbsp roughly chopped roasted peanuts

Lightly season the chicken breasts and saute them in 2 tbs groundnut oil until cooked through. Leave to cool.

Saute the spring onions, using a little more oil if you need to, in the same pan and put them in a broad flat bowl. Quickly fry the slices of garlic until golden – be really careful not to burn them. Add these to the bowl as well.

Cut the flesh from the mangoes - there is no need to peel it - and cut into lengths about the thickness of two matchsticks. Put these in the bowl along with the fish sauce, sugar and lime juice. Halve and deseed the chillies and slice them finely. Add to the bowl.

Finally cut the chicken into strips and add to the bowl with the herbs, watercress and 3½ tbs of groundnut oil. Mix everything together. Scatter the roasted peanuts over the top and serve.

Photo: Linda Maclean (stylist) John Lawrence Jones (photographer)

Insalata di Arance e Finocchio

Orange and Fennel Salad

This salad is typical of Sicily, where oranges are grown in abundance. It is eaten all over the south as well. I remember it was one of my father's favourite salads as a pre-lunch snack to refresh himself and stimulate his tastebuds – rather like an aperitif. The combination of sweet oranges, the aniseed flavour of the fennel and the saltiness of the anchovies make this a very tasty salad indeed.

4 oranges, peeled, all zest and pith removed
8 back olives, sliced
1 large fennel bulb, finely sliced (reserve the feathery fronds)
8 anchovy fillets
4 tbsp extra virgin olive oil
2 tsp red wine vinegar
salt and freshly ground black pepper

Take an orange in the palm of your hand and with a small, very sharp knife cut out the segments from between the membranes, discarding the pips and any pith still attached. Repeat with the remaining oranges.

Place the orange segments and sliced olives in a bowl. Then add the fennel and anchovies. Season with salt and pepper (be careful with the salt as the anchovies are already quite salty). Mix in the olive oil and vinegar, leave to marinate for a minute or two and then serve. Decorate with the green feathery leaves from the fennel.

Gennaro Contaldo

Gennaro Contaldo is one of the most respected chefs in London as well as a renowned personality in his own right. He is widely known as the Italian legend who taught Jamie Oliver all he knows about Italian cooking. Born in Minori on the Amalfi Coast, Gennaro's quintessentially Italian spirit and positive nature has made him a TV favourite. Gennaro has worked in some of London's most popular restaurants but in 1999 he opened his own restaurant 'Passione' in Charlotte Street, London. His first cookbook – also called Passione – was published by Headline in 2003, became winner of the 'Gourmand World Cookbook – Best Italian Cuisine Book 2003', and has been shortlisted for the Andre Simon Award.

Genevieve McGough

Genevieve McGough is a chef based in Auckland, with 16 years experience in professional cookery. She is also a self-taught photographer and photographs, as well as food-styles, all of the dishes for her cookbooks and recipe website, Genevieve's Cuisine. Her writing style is largely influenced by her solid technical background of classical training combined with the experience of working for some of Auckland's most innovative chefs. Her food writing specialises in turning professional, sometimes complex techniques into simple, easy to understand recipes for home cooks. Genevieve's first published cookbook is due for release by Penguin Books in May 2005.

Roast Jalapeño and Gourmet Potato Salad With Glazed Onions and Wasabi Dressing

Wasabi dressing

1 egg yolk
1 tbsp white wine vinegar
3 tbsp lemon juice
1 small glove garlic
1 tsp wasabi paste
1 tsp hot English mustard
¾ tsp salt
¾ cup soya bean oil

In a blender, place all the ingredients except the oil.

Turn the blender on to high speed.

Pour in a steady stream of oil but make the stream as thin as possible.

When all the oil is used up, the result should be a thin tangy mayonnaise.

To prepare the vegetables

2 Spanish onions
1 tbsp soft brown sugar
⅛ cup balsamic vinegar
4 jalapeños
1 tbsp olive oil
500g/1pound gourmet potatoes
Basil leaves
Cracked black pepper

Pre heat the oven to 180°C/350°F

Peel the Spanish onions and slice them through the core into 8 wedges.

Toss the onions in the brown sugar and balsamic vinegar then place into an ovenproof dish.

Roast the onions in a roasting pan for 20 minutes tossing occasionally then set aside until serving time.

Slice the jalapeños in half through the length.

Cut out the seeds and any white pith.

Place jalapeños onto an oiled baking tray skin side up and brush lightly with the olive oil.

Bake in the oven for 20 minutes.

If you have a fan oven, you can cook them at the same time as the onions.

Meanwhile, place the potatoes in a medium sized pot.

Cover with cold water and bring water to the boil.

Turn down the heat and simmer until the potatoes are just cooked, around 15 minutes from when the water starts to simmer.

Drain the potatoes and let them cool while you finish preparing the other vegetables.

To serve

Slice the potatoes into rounds.

On a large serving platter place on the vegetables attractively then drizzle over a little of the dressing. Lastly finish with picked basil leaves and cracked black pepper. Serves 2.

Notes

Notes

Andrew Jefford

Andrew Jefford, the son of a vicar and eldest of three brothers, grew up in Norfolk. He studied English at the University of Reading and pursued post-graduate studies with Malcolm Bradbury at the University of East Anglia before working as an editor for Paul Hamlyn's Octopus group. In the late 1980s he got the chance to combine his passions for wine and for writing, since then he has worked as a freelance drinks journalist and broadcaster, in particular for the *Evening Standard* and for BBC Radio Four. He has written eleven books and guides including the widely admired *The New France* and, in autumn 2004, *Peat Smoke and Spirit*. He has won a number of distinctions for his work, including 8 Glenfiddich Awards. He currently lives in Hastings.

Giving the Grain a Chance

Do you have an open palate or a closed one? Since you're reading this, I suspect it's the former rather than the latter. Closed palates exclude, eliminate and dismiss; what remains is a tight little circle of flavours and combinations whose main pleasure is provided by the reassurance of repetition. Open palates, by contrast, fling the windows wide, regardless of precedent or practice – and in flies pleasure, sometimes sporting unexpectedly colourful plumage.

Matching beer (rather than the habitual wine) with different foods is an excellent litmus test of the truly open palate. Most meals, in truth, could happily be partnered by either – and so could most fine raw ingredients. A trembling oyster, for example. Yes, that softly frilly flesh and those soothing marine juices are perfect with Chablis or Champagne – but they are every bit as good when they meet the charcoal profundities of **Guinness**. Moist, creamy roast beef is wonderful with a broad-shouldered red wine from the Southern Rhône like Châteauneuf du Pape, but it's no less striking with a great English regional ale like the cleansingly nutty Burton classic **Marston's Pedigree**. Roquefort and Sauternes is unctuously good, but Roquefort with **Fuller's** darkly explosive **Golden Pride** with its ricochets of citrus, toffee, burnt raisin and fresh hop bine, is every bit as memorably gratifying. Not better, remember, just different.

So why are so many palates closed to beer at mealtimes? Maybe it's the demon of bitterness. A mythical creature, by the way: not all beers are bitter, as you'll see in the next paragraph. Don't forget, too, that some of the world's greatest wines can also be bitter, particularly tannic reds and classic Italian reds. Bitterness which may seem superfluous or exaggerated in a glass of beer drunk on its own, moreover, suddenly makes perfect gastronomic sense when confronted with chunks of braised shank in a stew: it helps chase and harry the richness of a dish, and leave the mouth clean and fresh afterwards. In this sense, indeed, bitterness in beer serves much the same purpose as acidity in a wine.

If generously hopped, pungently bitter beers strike you as just too much of a good thing, then take a look at those beers designed to partner highly flavoured Indian and Asian foods. The unflappably grainy, smooth **Cobra**, for example, was created to accompany the spiced firework display of Indian dishes, which it does with calming success; another beer in the same mould is Thailand's **Singha** which, despite its higher strength of 6% abv (alcohol by volume), sets about the Machiavellian chillis and tangy fish gravy of Thai cooking with refreshing delicacy. Both, though, make good choices for those who prefer less assertively flavoured beers to partner vividly flavoured European-style foods like salads, pizzas and barbecued meats.

Beers like the Spanish **San Miguel**, full of smoothly bittersweet malt, or the darker, toastier **Samuel Adams Boston Lager** occupy the middle ground in the battle between those drinkers who like a cascade of bitter notes with their dinner and those who'd rather enjoy the softer, creamier pleasures of gentle grain. San Miguel is a satisfying beer to chose with tuna steaks, for example, especially if you're going to cook them (as a Spanish chef might) in an earthenware dish with tomatoes, peppers and garlic. The same dish works well with Boston Lager, too, though maybe buttery braised cod with chicory is even better. (Boston, remember, was the nearest large city to the now exhausted Grand Banks, once the greatest cod fishery in the world.)

Shepherd Neame, Britain's oldest brewer, also strikes a seaside note with its **Whitstable Bay Organic Ale**: a fine, fragrant, blond beer of the kind which is currently winning over many former lager drinkers. Seafood devotees will know Whitstable as the source of some of Britain's best oysters; personally, though, I like this coolly quenching ale best with scallops and prawn dishes, or baked fish served with samphire. Crisp, lager-style beers are also excellent with white fish and salmon, especially the pale pink but flavoury organic versions sold by Waitrose. If your palate is as open as I suspect it might be, then you won't need me to tell you that the Czech Republic is the source of some of the world's greatest lagers, such as the sinewy, pungent, almost piney **Pilsner Urquell** (or 'original source' – this was the beer that gave the name 'Pils' to the world).

What about something richer? You won't find any beer more lushly flavour-laden than **Liefman's Kriek.** If you allow 100 litres of strong Belgian ale to spend six months in bed (or barrel) with 13kg of sweet Danish cherries and smaller, drier, tarter Belgian Kriek cherries, this foaming and fragrant fruit beer is the result. I generally serve it as an aperitif, but it does drink surprisingly well with rich duck, goose or pork dishes, too: you might almost believe it's wine. Even stronger, though much drier, is the surprisingly pale but powerfully aromatic **Duvel**, a blue-blooded aristocrat of the beer shelves and the one-sip proof that beer can be every bit as complex as wine. It's another great choice for roast duck or goose, and its also a fine foil to the oily fish we're all meant to be eating more of like plump, steel-flanked mackerel or the bright and silvery herring.

Who said the beer world lacked variety? In the end, though, we all boomerang back to the classics. I love roast chicken, for example, slivers of garlic oven-softened under its butter-brown skin, with a dish of rough-edged roast potatoes. This is the time to return to the great ales of England, heavy-boughed with country scent and flavour, and nothing could be better for that chicken than a motherly 750ml bottle of the nourishingly multi-layered **Old Speckled Hen**.

Previously published in *Waitrose Food Illustrated*

FISH

Koluu (Hema Lallindre Ranawake)

Koluu, as we all know him, is undoubtedly Sri Lanka's domestic god. Food, as he creates it, is out of this world, and a feast for both eye and palate. His love of food, and creating innovative repasts, which was a hobby since his school days, has now become a profession. His mother, who was a good cook, probably inspired him. Koluu ventured into the world, working as a chef for Ambassadors of various countries, first in Iraq and then in Portugal, catering for the rich and famous in and around that country. After a few years, in which he gathered considerable international experience adding to his repertoire of gourmet cooking, he decided to return home and start his own restaurants. These were an instant success, noted for their high standard of food and ambiance; he runs Frangipani, Tulips and Barefoot, all popular with both young and old.

Ilica Karunaratne, Columnist

Sauteed Prawns with Spices Done 'Tulips' Style

8 large prawns
3 tbsp vegetable oil
1 stalk lemon grass (cleaned)
4 medium sized onions
5 cloves of garlic
chunk of fresh ginger (2 inches)
3 tbsp ground coriander powder
2 tsp Indian saffron (turmeric)
1 tbsp desiccated coconut
A sprig of curry leaves or 3 bay leaves
¼ tsp salt
12oz cream
1 tbsp Chinese sweet chilli sauce
3 tbsp brown sugar
50g almonds or cashewnuts
50g fresh coriander leaves

Clean and devein prawns leaving the tails on.

Heat 2 tablespoons of oil in a frying pan or wok over moderate heat and when hot toss the prawns in and cook for about 1½ minutes. Remove from pan and set aside.

In the meantime, chop the lemon grass and drop into the food processor or grinder along with the onions, garlic, ginger, coconut and almonds and grind to a paste. If necessary, use a tablespoon of water when grinding.

In the same pan add remaining oil and heat the pan. Then add the bay/curry leaves, paste, saffron, coriander powder, chilli sauce and salt and cook together. Thereafter add the cream into the paste and the sugar. When gravy is smooth, add in the prawns and cook for a further minute. Take off the fire and place in a dish and garnish with chopped coriander leaves.

This is best served with steamed white rice.

Photo: Asanga Dissanayake

Squid Stir Fried with Sweet Cumin and Lime Juice

Fritz Zwahlen

6 whole squid with tentacles
2 tsp sweet cumin powder
1 tsp coriander powder
2 tsp sea salt
1 tsp fenugreek
8 tbsp coconut oil or vegetable oil
1 whole red onion peeled and sliced
2 whole green chillies sliced with the seeds in
4 pc dried red chilli whole
1 clove garlic sliced finely
5cm ginger root, peeled and sliced in to julienne
12 curry leaves
100ml coconut cream
2 limes juiced

Clean the squid and slice into 1cm thick pieces lengthways.

Rub the squid with the dried spices and set aside.

Heat the oil in a large heavy based frying pan and fry the onions and garlic until just browned.

Add the curry leaves, ginger, chillies and fry for a few seconds.

Add the marinated squid and continue to fry over a high heat until just cooked.

Add coconut cream and remove from the heat.

Add lime juice to taste.

Serve with a small salad of chopped cucumber, tomato, red onion, green chilli and coriander tossed with lime juice.

Shanth Fernando

Shanth Fernando, the designer and proprietor of Paradise Road, is known by many of his followers as the 'style guru' and named by *Wallpaper Magazine* as 'Sri Lanka's own Terence Conran'. Paradise Road is made up of four design stores, The Gallery Café (listed as one of Asia's top restaurants in *East Magazine* and referred to by *Condé Nast Magazine* as 'the only place to eat in Colombo') and Paradise Road Galleries. In his hotel training, Shanth worked in hotel kitchens in the Netherlands and also sat with management on menu planning.

Grilled Prawns with Papaya and Carrot Salad on Coconut Risotto

Serves 2

10 Tiger Prawns

Marinade

2 tbsp lime juice
½ tsp paprika
1 tsp crushed garlic
dash of fish sauce
1 pinch sea salt
2 pinches freshly ground black pepper

Risotto

250g Arborio Rice
350ml vegetable stock, warmed
50ml white wine
1 clove garlic, chopped
½ onion, finely chopped
100ml thick coconut milk
Salt and pepper to taste
2 coriander leaves for garnish

For the salad

1 large wedge of papaya
1 large carrot
2 tsp lime juice
1 tsp honey
1 tsp tomato ketchup
dash of balsamic vinegar

Devein and shell the prawns. Place all the marinade ingredients in a bowl, add the prawns, cover and refrigerate for one hour.

To prepare the risotto sauté the garlic and onions in olive oil, add the rice and fry till glassy. Gradually add the warmed vegetable stock and wine, cook till al dente, stirring constantly. Add the coconut milk, stir well and cook for two more minutes.

Julienne the carrot and papaya. Mix the remainder of the ingredients in a bowl and combine with the carrot and papaya. Refrigerate until needed.

Grill the prawns for 3 minutes on each side and serve with the risotto and salad garnished with one coriander leaf.

Crab Risotto with Coconut Milk and Coriander

Fresh crab and coconut milk add a luxurious richness to Ross Burden's stylish fusion-inspired risotto.

Serves 4 • preparation 15 minutes • cooking 30 minutes

3 tbsp sunflower oil
1 medium onion, finely chopped
3 garlic cloves, finely chopped
450g risotto rice
1 litre fish stock, (more if necessary)
400ml coconut milk
5 fresh limes leaves, finely shredded
250g fresh cooked white crab meat
15g fresh coriander, chopped
freshly ground black pepper

Heat the sunflower oil in a heavy-based medium saucepan. Add in the onion and garlic and fry gently until softened, around 5 minutes.

Add in the risotto rice and fry for a further 2 minutes, stirring.

Meanwhile, bring the fish stock to the boil in a separate saucepan.

Slowly add the boiling stock, a ladleful at a time, to the rice, cooking and stirring for about 5-10 minutes to allow each addition to be absorbed before adding the next.

Once the stock has been completely absorbed, gradually add in the coconut milk in the same way as the stock.

Cook the risotto until the grains of rice are still firm but not chalky, using as much coconut milk as possible and more fish stock if necessary. The finished risotto should be on the wet side.

When the rice is almost done, stir through the lime leaves, crabmeat and coriander.

Season well with plenty of black pepper. Serve at once.

Taken from www.uktvfood.co.uk

Ross Burden

Once described as 'The tastiest man in Britain', Ross Burden has been a feature on British screens for eight years. The model turned presenter has hosted and guested on many shows here, in NZ, USA, South Africa and across Asia. He is best known for being adept in the kitchen on shows such as *Masterchef* and *Ready, Steady Cook*. Ross is a trained naturalist and keen traveller. A degree in Zoology and an upbringing on the New Zealand coast have equipped him to explore the natural world for *National Geographic*. In his spare time Ross loves to travel, with Asia as a favourite destination.

Aldo Zilli

Lobster in Orange and Chilli with Mustard Mashed Potatoes

A lobster doesn't need a lot of attention. It can be simply boiled, split open and served with mayonnaise and salad, or buy it ready-cooked. It's a great dish for the summertime. If you're after something a bit more involved and with an adventurous taste, then this is the recipe you've been looking for.

Serves 4 • preparation 40 minutes • cooking 25 minutes

For the mashed potatoes
4 large potatoes, washed
30ml (2 tbsp) Dijon mustard
20ml (4 tsp) butter
10ml (2 tsp) double cream
5ml (1 tsp) freshly grated Parmesan cheese
salt and freshly ground black pepper

For the lobsters
4 x 450g (1lb) cooked lobsters
30g (1oz) butter
1 fresh red chilli, seeded and finely chopped
1 shallot, finely chopped
5ml (1 tsp) brown sugar
juice of 2 oranges
2 oranges, peeled and segmented
15ml (1 tbsp) Grand Marnier

For the garnish (optional)
125g (4½ oz) granulated sugar
1 orange, thinly sliced

Prick the potatoes with a skewer or fork, place in a pan of salted water and bring to the boil. Cook for 15–20 minutes until tender. Drain, and when cool enough to handle, peel the potatoes and mash in a large bowl with a potato masher. Stir in the mustard, butter, cream and Parmesan cheese and season to taste. Set aside and keep warm.

Meanwhile, cut the lobsters in half and remove the meat. Reserve the shells for presentation.

Melt the butter in small pan, add the chilli and shallot and sauté for 5 minutes until tender but not brown. Add the brown sugar and orange juice and cook for 2–3 minutes until the sauce thickens.

Stir the lobster meat and orange segments into the sauce and cook for

3 minutes. Add the Grand Marnier and season to taste. Simmer for 1 further minute.

If making the garnish, put the granulated sugar in a heavy-based pan and heat gently until the sugar dissolves, then cook for 2–3 minutes until the sugar turns to a golden caramel.

Meanwhile, pre-heat the grill to hot. Place the orange slices under the grill to dry out a little. Dip the orange slices in the caramel and set aside to set.

Fill the lobster shells with the mashed potatoes and place on hot serving plates. Spoon the lobster meat on to the mashed potatoes, then drizzle the sauce over the lobster. Garnish with the caramelized orange slices, if desired. Serve immediately.

Taken from *Zilli Fish* by Aldo Zilli

Pat Chapman

Kakuluo

Sri Lankan Crab Curry

The most common crab in the Indian Ocean is the long clawed blue crab (ketam biru). The huge green crab is also popular. There are numerous other crabs, in various parts of the world, all yielding tasty flesh. This Sri Lankan recipe combines crab flesh in a creamy thick paste to create a delicious curry.

Serves 4

4 cooked crabs (any type) each weighing about 450g
1 tbsp vegetable oil
2 tbsp sesame oil
1 tbsp fresh coriander leaves, chopped
aromatic salt to taste
400ml coconut milk
1 cupful cooked plain rice

Garnish

some onion tarka
some fresh curry leaves
lime wedges

The Paste

2-4 garlic cloves, minced
4 or 5 spring onions (scallions) bulbs and leaves chopped
1 to 3 fresh red chillies, chopped
75g / 1 cupful fresh coconut flesh

Spices

mustard seeds
sesame seeds
curry leaves, fresh

Combine the paste ingredients and mulch down in the blender using just enough water to achieve a pourable paste.

Extract all the flesh you can from the pincers, claws and legs as well as the body.

Heat the oils in your karahi or wok. Stir-fry the spices for 20 seconds. Add the paste and stir-fry for about 4 to 5 minutes.

Add the crab meat and leaves and sufficient water to prevent it sticking. Salt to taste.

Garnish and serve with rice.

Stir-fried Peppers with Scallops

Scallops are fragile, sweetly delicate morsels and need very little preparation or cooking time. They embody the virtues of "quick, easy, delicious." In this recipe, I combine them with nutritious, flavourful, and colourful red and green peppers. The result is a festive looking dish that belies its ease of preparation. Perfect for a family meal or as the centrepiece of a dinner party prepared at short notice.

Serves 4-6 • preparation 15 minutes • cooking 10 minutes

1lb (450g) fresh scallops
8oz (225g) red peppers, about 2
4oz (100g) green pepper, about 1
1½ tbsp oil, preferably groundnut
1½ tbsp spring onions, coarsely chopped
1 tbsp garlic, coarsely chopped
2 tsp fresh ginger, finely chopped
Sauce
1 tbsp light soy sauce
2 tsp yellow bean sauce
2 tbsp rice wine or dry sherry
1 tsp sugar
1 tsp sesame oil

Dry the scallops with kitchen paper and set aside. Cut the peppers into 1 inch (2.5cm) squares.

Heat a wok or large frying pan until it is hot, then add the oil, spring onions, garlic, and ginger, and stir-fry for 10 seconds. Then add the peppers and stir-fry for 2 minutes. Stir in the scallops and the sauce ingredients. Continue to cook for another 4 minutes. Serve at once.

Hint:
** You can substitute asparagus, courgettes, or mange-tout for the peppers.*
** If you like very spicy food, add 2 fresh chillies to this recipe.*
** Variations for this recipe: use mussels or clams instead of scallops.*

Taken from *Quick & Easy Chinese Cooking* 1985

Ken Hom

Ken Hom is widely regarded as one of the world's greatest authorities on oriental cooking and travels extensively to demonstrate his culinary skills. He has made several series for the BBC including *Hot Wok*, *Travels with a Hot Wok* and *Foolproof Chinese Cookery*. His book *Chinese Cookery* has sold over a million copies. He is also the author of the award-winning *Easy Family Dishes: A Memoir with Recipes* and several other recipe books. Ken Hom is a director of Noble House Leisure Limited which includes the Yellow River Cafés and other restaurants. He lives in London, Paris, south-west France and Bangkok.

Photo: © David Loftus 2004

Tuna Carpaccio – Japanese Style

This is a wonderfully simple, almost exotic, light meal that fills you with a big smile. For the tuna, try to get bluefin or bigeye, but yellowfin can be really good as well. Your tuna needs to be red and almost waxy-looking. You can try using different fish, such as salmon, bream or scallops, just make sure they're all really nice and fresh and smell of nothing but the sea.

Serves 2

200g fresh tuna, in one piece
small piece of mooli (white Asian radish) or a handful of radishes
1 small red chilli, halved and deseeded
purple shiso cress leaves* or coriander sprigs (optional)
1 lime, halved
soy sauce
olive oil, to drizzle

Get your tuna, and with a long sharp knife slice it as thinly as you can. Once you've sliced it, you can smooth it over with the side of your knife to make it even thinner. Divide this in one layer between your plates, or it's even nicer to serve it on one big plate.

Next, use this brilliant Japanese trick: cut a V-shaped vertical slit in the mooli and stuff the chilli in. This means that when you grate it you get a pink-coloured, chilli-flavoured radish pulp, which is fantastic. If you haven't got mooli you can get the same effect by finely chopping the chilli and grating normal radishes. So, either grate or chop your mooli or radish and then blob it and its juice over the tuna slices and sprinkle over the shiso or coriander. When you serve it to your loved one at the table, all they need to do is squeeze half a lime and a couple of teaspoons of soy sauce to their own taste equally over the fish, then drizzle with a little olive oil.

** Shiso is a Japanese herb with a strong flavour reminiscent of aniseed*

© Jamie Oliver 2004
www.jamieoliver.com

Jamie Oliver

Photo: © David Loftus 2004

Jamie Oliver started cooking in his parents' pub, The Cricketers, in Clavering, Essex, at the age of eight. He has since worked with some of the world's top chefs and is now running Fifteen – one of the best restaurants in London. Jamie has written five bestselling cookery books that have sold over 11 million copies worldwide. His many award-winning television series have been sold in over 46 countries. He currently writes for *News of the World* in the UK, *Delicious* magazine in the UK and Australia and *Tip* magazine in Holland. He also started and continues to be involved with the charity Fifteen Foundation, which allows disadvantaged youngsters to follow their dreams and become chefs. Jamie lives in London with his wife and two daughters.

Pat Chapman

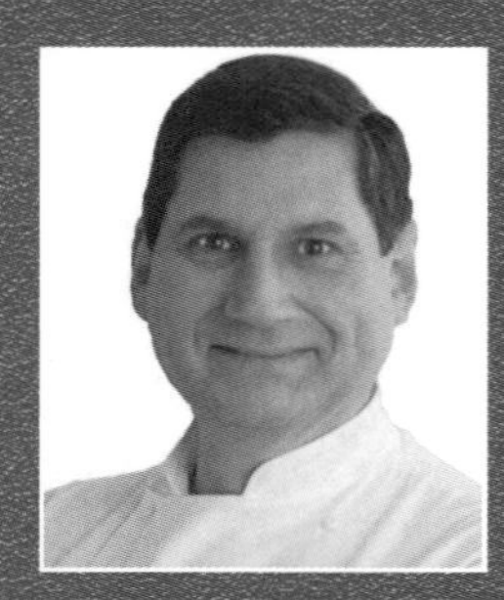

Fihunu Mas Lebai

Andaman Grilled Garlic Fish

The Andamans are a group of Indian islands in the Indian ocean, off Burma. Fish is inevitable and this garlic and chilli-coated recipe is ideal for the barbecue. I've given a recipe for the grill which is well worth trying, though it does make the house smell garlicky. Try it with whole fresh red mullet, known locally as Lebai.

Serves 4

4 whole red mullet, about 30cm long, gutted
1 cupful fresh lime juice
1 tsp aromatic salt
2 tsp finely chopped red chillies
8 garlic cloves, minced
6oz (175g) 1 cupful chopped cashew nuts
1 tbsp chopped fresh coriander leaves
2 or 3 fresh green chillies, chopped
1 tbsp sesame oil

Wash and dry the fish. Make several slashes in the side of the fish with a sharp knife.

Mix the lime juice, salt and chilli together. Coat the fish, inside and out and leave to stand for an hour or so, in the fridge.

Meanwhile, put the garlic, nuts, coriander leaves, chillies and oil into the food processor or blender, using enough water to achieve a smooth pourable paste.

Rub the paste onto both sides of the fish. (Retain any spare paste).

Preheat the grill to medium. Line pan with foil to catch drips. Put the fish in the pan rack and under the heat at the midway position. Grill for 8-10 minutes.

Turn and grill for a further 5-8 minutes. Baste with any remaining paste. Serve, garnished with lime wedges and salad.

Pat Chapman

Malacca Ikan Manis

Indonesian Sweet and Sour Fish

From Indonesia, the original home of the clove, mace and nutmeg, comes this fish dish in an aromatic sweet and sour sauce.

Serves 4

4 fresh mackerel about 350g each, cleaned
2-4 fresh green chillies, whole
1 or 2 stalks fresh lemon grass
400ml milk
1 tbsp tamarind purée
1 tbsp brown sugar
2 tsp ketjap manis (sweet soy sauce)
2 tsp sambal manis (sweet chilli sauce)
200ml coconut milk
1 tbsp chopped fresh mint leaves
aromatic salt to taste

1/2 tsp freshly grated nutmeg
6-8 whole cloves,
1 tsp whole mace, crushed
8cm cinnamon stick

Garnish

2 tbsp pan-roasted peanuts, chopped
some fresh coriander leaves

Spices

Place the fish, chillies and lemon grass into a suitable-sized lidded casserole dish.

Mix the milk, tamarind, brown sugar, ketjap and sambal manis and spices together. Pour it over the fish and put the casserole, lid-on, into the oven preheated to 190°C / 375°F /Gas Mark 5.

Cook for 30 minutes. Add the coconut milk and fresh mint. Cook for about 15 minutes more. Salt to taste.

Garnish with the nuts and chives.

Grilled King Prawn Jakarta-style

Serves 5

100g Kedondong (tropical fruit)
100g Finely sliced cabbage
100g Finely sliced Bangkuang (tropical fruit)
50g Bean sprouts
1 pc Pineapple – diced
100g Cucumber – diced
150g Shredded carrot
50g French Lettuce
1 pc 'Kerupuk Kuning' (Indonesian typical chips/crackers)
80g Peanuts
20g Red Chilli
20g Dried Shrimps
175ml Vinegar
500ml Water
150g Sugar
15g Salt
30g Garlic
5 pcs King Prawn

Peel the prawns, leave the tail, clean it, then marinate with salt and pepper. Grill till cooked, set aside.

Marinate the fruits and vegetables in water, add some salt and sugar. Leave it for a moment, then strain.

Fry the 'kerupuk kuning' and peanuts, set aside.

Boil with some water: the sugar, red chilli, garlic, dried shrimps and carrots, add the vinegar. Blend with mixer, then strain.

Mix the fruits and vegetables with some of the blended chilli, garlic, carrots and dried shrimps, then mix well with some boiled water. Leave it for 6 hours in the refrigerator.

Put the Asinan / pickled fruits & vegetables in the plate, garnish with French lettuce, peanuts and 'Kerupuk Kuning', then put the prawn on top.

William Wongso

William Wongso is a famous Indonesian restaurateur. His love of food and wine has lead him to train in Sydney, California and France. His highest achievement throughout his career was when he received an award given by the French Ministry of Agriculture called 'Chevalier dans l'Ordre du Merite Agricole'. This was awarded by the French government upon William's effort in promoting the French culinary and gastronomy tradition. William's interest in wine grew along with his passion for food. Having undertaken a Californian Wine Education Program at the University of California, Davis he is the current President of the Jakarta branch of the International Wine & Food Society.

Red Mullet with Deep-fried Rocket and Toasted Sesame Seeds

James Martin

Serves 2

2 x 75g (6oz) red mullet fillets
(skin on but no bones)
Oil for deep frying
115g (4oz) rocket leaves
Salt and freshly ground
black pepper
2 tbsp olive oil
25g (1oz) sesame seeds, toasted

Most fish, including red mullet, are available all year round, but the best season for this particular fish is from June or July to September. Avoid small fish which are fiddly to prepare and contain a lot of tiny bones. If you can't get larger fish use salmon fillets instead as there really isn't much point in persevering with red mullet that are too tiny. Serve the fish with plain boiled new potatoes. The simple flavours work together amazingly well. Alternatively, roast new potatoes in some garlic cloves, thyme, olive oil and rock salt for about 45 minutes on a high heat.

Place the red mullet fillets on a flat surface, skin side up, and with a sharp knife make about eight small slashes in the skin. Be careful not to cut through the whole width of the skin – leave about 5mm (¼ inch) on either side of the fillet.

Heat the oil in a deep pan or fryer to a high heat. Don't wash the rocket, but place it in the fryer in two batches: this is to prevent the fat from overflowing as, when you add the rocket, it will bubble up, so be careful. Keep your eye on the rocket, and remove from the fryer once the leaves go translucent. Don't over-cook as the rocket will taste bitter; under-cooking will prevent the leaves crisping up. Once you have removed them from the fryer, place on some kitchen paper to drain, and season with a little salt.

Heat a non-stick pan to a high heat on the stove with the olive oil. Season the mullet fillets and place in the pan, skin side down, and cook for about 2 minutes, until the skin is nice and crispy. Then turn them over and cook for about 1 minute.

Divide the crisp rocket between two plates. Place the red mullet fillets, skin side up, in the middle of the rocket, sprinkle with some of the toasted sesame seeds. Serve.

Fritz Zwahlen

Grilled Snapper with Tomato Sambol

1 whole red snapper or reef fish approx 2kg

Scale and clean the fish. Fill the cavity with broken lemon grass stalks and pandan leaves. Make incisions on both sides of the fish at 2 cm intervals, rub the fish with salt and cook over a hot charcoal fire for approximately 15 minutes on each side.

Serve with yellow rice, warm tomato sambol, sliced lime and coriander leaves.

Tomato sambol

200g sweet ripe tomatoes roughly chopped
100g green tomatoes roughly chopped
4 whole small red onions peeled and sliced
6 cloves garlic sliced
2 whole green chillies sliced with the seeds in
5cm ginger root, peeled and sliced into julienne
12 curry leaves
1 tbsp curry powder
1 tsp mustard seeds
1 tsp fennel seeds
6 cardamom pods
1 stick cinnamon
8 cloves
100ml vegetable oil
300ml coconut milk

Cut the tomatoes into large pieces.

Heat the oil in a large heavy based frying pan and fry the onions and garlic until just browned.

Add the curry leaves, ginger, chillies and spices , fry for a few seconds.

Add the tomatoes and curry powder and fry for a further 2 minutes.

Add coconut milk and reduce the heat to a low simmer.

Cook for 10 minutes and remove from heat.

Add salt to taste.

Ian Pengelley

Ian Pengelley's restaurant 'Pengelley's' at 164 Sloane St, SW1 specialises in New Asian Cuisine. Ian started cooking at sixteen years of age in England before moving to Hong Kong where he learnt Asian style cooking. His grasp of Cantonese helped enormously in gaining work experience at restaurants around China, Thailand and Singapore. He has extensively researched the cuisine of South East Asia for the Pengelley menu and has enjoyed a stint living with a Thai family for one-to-one intensive tuition. Ian has appeared in various shows and television programmes. He is a keen runner and takes part in the London Marathon.

Smoked Ocean Trout, Starfruit, Green Mango and Thai Herbs

Ocean Trout; scaled and cleaned
1½ cups of Grated coconut
1 cup of Jasmine rice
1 cup of Lap son sou choung tea

Score the fish. (Marinade trout in light soy sauce, sugar, a little white pepper for 1 hour). Mix ingredients together. Line a wok with foil, place mix into the foil. Put the fish 'standing up' in a rack in the wok. Place the wok on a high heat. When it smokes, turn down the heat and cover. Smoke for 30mins – 1 hour.

Salad

½ cup Sweet Basil
1 tbsp Pak Chi Farang
½ cup Coriander
½ cup Vietnamese Mint (torn)
½ cup Bean sprouts
½ cup Julienne spring onions
1 Green mango – thin batons
1 Star fruit (sliced down the edges of the star to make thin strips.)
Oil for frying

Dressing

1 Bird'seye chilli
4 Shallots
4 Green chillies – seeded
4 Coriander Roots
4 Garlic cloves
Palm sugar
Lime juice
Fish sauce
Pinch of sea salt

Smash the garlic, shallots, coriander roots and chillies to a pulp in a mortar and pestle. Add salt. Add palm sugar, lime juice and fish sauce. It should taste sour, hot and a little salty. Take the cooled down trout. Peel off large chunks. Deep fry until crispy.

Place trout chunks in a bowl and add star fruit strips. Add 1 tbsp of herbs. Add 4 tbsp of sauce. Serve.

Green Thai Fish Curry

Thai curries are incredibly easy to make, very quick to cook and totally delicious. The secret is in the mixture of spices and the freshness of the pastes which are traditionally made with a pestle and mortar. Alternatively make the paste in a food processor using ground spices.

Serves 4

Spice Paste

1 onion sliced
3 garlic cloves cut up
6 small hot green chilli deseeded and sliced
5cm fresh ginger scraped and sliced
1 tsp white pepper ground
1 tsp coriander ground
½ tsp turmeric ground
½ tsp cumin ground
1 tsp shrimp paste (belacan)
1 tbsp fish sauce
1 stalk of lemon grass peeled and sliced thinly

750g fish fillets, such as cod, haddock, John Dory or other firm fish
1 tbsp of peanut oil
400ml coconut milk
1 tbsp fresh coriander, chopped

To Serve

sprigs of Thai basil
2 limes, quartered
fragrant Thai rice or noodles

Place all the spice paste ingredients in the food processor and work them into a fine puree. Set aside.

Put the oil in a wok and heat well. Add the spice paste and stir fry for a few seconds to release the aromas. Add the thick portion from the top of the coconut milk, stir well and boil to thicken a little.

Add the fish and turn the pieces over in the sauce until they are well coated. Reheat to simmering point and cook until they start to become opaque. About two minutes.

Add the remaining coconut milk and chopped coriander and continue cooking until the fish is ready. Serve topped with Thai basil plus the halved limes and fragrant Thai rice or noodles.

Taken from *'Casseroles'* published by Ryland Peters & Small 2001

Sonia Stevenson

Sonia Stevenson, a Master Chef for 25 years, founded and ran her own restaurant, The Horn of Plenty, in Devon. She was the first woman in Britain to be awarded a Michelin star. She has cooked as a visiting chef in many famous restaurants (including being the first woman allowed to prepare one of her dishes in the kitchens of Maxims in Paris), taught in a number of cookery schools and has appeared on many television programmes. Travelling the country giving demonstrations or holding short specialized cookery courses are her main occupations as well as writing cookery books in her spare time.

Anjum Anand

Anjum Anand grew up in London and studied in London, Geneva, Paris and Madrid; she has a BA in European Business Administration. Since then she has turned her hand to her passion for cooking and, in particular, making her native Indian food lighter and heathier. Anjum has worked in the trend-setting Cafe Spice in New York, for Tommy Tang and the Mondrian Hotel in Los Angeles as well as the Park Royal Hotel's Indian restaurant in New Delhi. She has travelled extensively in India learning about regional eating habits, foods and dishes. She has cooked on the BBC's *Good Food Live* Show and lives in London.

Mangalorian Fish Curry
Mangalori Machchi

Serves 4-5

1 tsp vegetable oil
½ small onion, finely sliced
2 small tomatoes, each cut into 8 sections
½ tsp ginger paste
1 green chilli, left whole
1 tsp paprika
salt to taste
½ tsp turmeric
5 tbsp coconut milk powder
150ml (5fl oz) hot water
25g (¾oz) block of tamarind, soaked and juice extracted (see below) or to taste
2-3 large fish steaks, cut into 4-6 portions

Paste

½ onion, roughly chopped
3 fat garlic cloves
2.5cm (1 inch) piece of fresh ginger, peeled
½ tsp cumin seeds
1 good pinch each of brown mustard seeds and black peppercorns
1½ tbsp coriander seeds or powder
2 –3 large mild red chillies, seeded and roughly chopped
100ml (3½fl oz) hot water

First, make the paste. Put all the paste ingredients except the water into a blender or food processor, and process, adding the water slowly, until you have a very fine and fluffy paste. Set aside.

Heat the oil in a large non-stick saucepan and fry the onion for 1 minute. Add the tomatoes, ginger paste, chilli, paprika, salt and turmeric. Stir-fry for 2 minutes. Add the paste and cook, covered, over a moderate heat for 10-12 minutes.

Add the coconut powder together with the water. Bring to the boil and then simmer for 5 minutes. Add the tamarind juice to taste.

Add the fish and swirl the pan to coat it thoroughly. Cook at a moderate to high heat for 5–6 minutes or until the fish is done. Adjust the seasoning and liquid content. The gravy should be creamy but not thick.

continued overleaf

Photo: Siân Irvine

IMLI KA PASTE

Tamarind paste

Tamarind is sold in died blocks, as a paste and as a concentrate. I always choose the block form as it keeps well and I feel I have more control over the ingredient. The paste, used judiciously, works just as well but I suggest that you avoid the concentrate as it is very powerful and can easily ruin a dish.

To extract the juice from the tamarind, cut 2.5 – 5 cm (1 – 2 inches) off the block and cover with 4cm (1½ inches) of hot water. Leave for 15 – 20 minutes to soften. Using a fork, mash the softened pulp into the water. Squeeze the solids to extract all the juice and discard together with the pods, or pass through a sieve. If you wish, you can make a paste from the whole block and store it in an ice-cube tray in the freezer where it will keep for several months.

Sugar-seared Tuna with Sticky Rice Cakes, Choi Sum and Ginger–lime Ponzu

Paul Gayler

Marinating fish in brown sugar or palm sugar is a favourite trick of mine as it gives it a beautifully caramelised exterior. Ponzu, a Japanese dipping sauce used for sashimi, sushi and other dishes, makes a good, tart contrast. It is very simple to prepare and wonderfully tasty. A word of advice would be to make a large amount of it, since you'll find yourself looking for more – it really is good! Try it with all manner of grilled seafood.

Serves 4

4 x 200g (7oz) tuna fillets
400g (14oz) cooked sushi rice (or other glutinous rice)
6 spring onions, finely shredded
350g (12oz) choi sum (Chinese flowering cabbage)
2 tbsp sesame oil
4 tbsp vegetable oil

For the marinade:
50g (2oz) brown sugar
1 tbsp nam pla (Thai fish sauce)
1 tbsp sweet chilli sauce
1 garlic clove, crushed
2.5cm (1 inch) piece of fresh root ginger, finely grated
Juice of ½ lime

For the ginger–lime ponzu
Juice of 1 lime
2 tbsp rice vinegar
4cm (1½ inch) piece of fresh root ginger, finely chopped
2 tbsp dark soy sauce
1 tbsp mirin (Japanese sweet rice wine)
100ml (3½ fl oz) well-flavoured chicken stock
1 tbsp chopped coriander

continued overleaf

To make the marinade, gently heat the sugar in a pan until dissolved, then add 150ml (¼ pint) of water and bring to the boil. Boil for 2 minutes, until sticky in consistency. Add the nam pla and chilli sauce and cook for 1 minute, then pour into a bowl. Stir in the garlic, ginger and lime juice and leave to cool. Place the tuna steaks in the marinade, turning to coat them, and leave for 2 hours.

In a bowl, combine the cooked rice with 4 of the spring onions and shape into 4 patties, about 7.5cm (3 inch) in diameter and 2cm (¾ inch) high. Steam the choi sum and season with half the sesame oil and some salt and pepper. Keep warm.

Heat the vegetable oil in a large frying pan until almost smoking. Remove the tuna from the marinade, add to the pan and fry quickly for about 1 minute on each side, until browned and caramelised. Remove from the pan and keep warm. Fry the spring onion cakes in the remaining sesame oil until golden and crisp.

For the ponzu, simply place all the ingredients in a pan and bring to boiling point, then remove from the heat.

To serve, arrange a spring onion cake on each serving plate, drape over the choi sum and top with the caramelised tuna. Sprinkle over the ponzu dressing and the remaining spring onions and serve immediately.

Notes

Notes

Tim Atkin

Tim Atkin MW is one of Britain's leading wine writers and an internationally recognised expert on the subject. He is the wine correspondent of *The Observer,* where he appears every Sunday in *OM*, and Wine Editor at Large of *Off Licence News*. He also writes for *Decanter*, *WINE International*, *Woman and Home* and *Observer Food Monthly*. He has presented the wine series, Grape Expectations, on the Carlton Food Network, and has appeared on Newsnight, Sky News, UK Good Food Live and Channel 5's Espresso as well as on numerous radio shows.

Do women taste better than men? Sorry, I'll rephrase that to avoid any hint of innuendo. Are women better wine tasters than men?

The commonly held image of a wine expert may be jowly, pinstriped and male – two parts Falstaff to one part City banker – but the person pronouncing on the merits of a bottle of vino, whether on television, in the press or as a professional buyer or auctioneer, is increasingly likely to be female. The head of Sotheby's wine department is a woman, at least three of the wine teams at the major supermarkets are run by women and the wine columns of The Times, The Financial Times, The Guardian and The Sunday Times are all penned by women. Popular prejudice may indicate otherwise – how often does a waiter hand the wine list to a woman in a restaurant? – but a female wine expert is not a contradiction in terms.

Indeed, there is scientific evidence to suggest that women are physically more capable tasters than men. Who says so? None other than Professor Linda Bartoshuk of Yale University's School of Medicine, who has studied sensory science for the past 25 years. She says: 'As a rule, women are born better tasters and learn to be better smellers than men. The world tastes more intense to women than it does to men.'

What evidence is there to support her claim? To find out, we need to make the acquaintance of something called propylthiouracil, or PTU for short, which is used in the treatment of thyroid disorders. This bitter-tasting compound is used by Bartoshuk to divide the world into non-tasters, tasters and super-tasters. She soaks pieces of blotting paper in PTU and hands them out to human guinea pigs. Roughly a quarter of them taste nothing when they place the blotting paper on their tongues, half perceive a degree of bitterness, while the remainder (the so-called super-tasters) taste something intensely bitter.

Such a perception may be genetic and is almost certainly related to the number of taste buds on the tongue. These can vary in density from as few as 11 per square centimetre to as many as 1,100, depending on the individual. No prizes for guessing that the more taste buds, the more sensitive the tongue. Or that, according to Bartoshuk, women are more likely to be super-tasters than men. Bartoshuk says that 35 per cent of women are born super-tasters, compared with 15 per cent of men, and that 10 per cent of women are 'more sensitive to taste than any man'.

Another blow struck for the fairer sex? Before female readers get over-excited, I should point out that taste is only one of four senses involved in the appreciation and assessment of wine (sight, touch and smell being the other three). And that bitterness (tannin in wine) is only one flavour.

Let me explain further. Taste is a comparatively blunt instrument as it can identify only four, or possibly five, things: bitterness, saltiness, sweetness and sourness. The fifth taste is umami, a Japanese term that means 'savoury' and refers to the taste of amino acids. Some people call this the 'taste-good factor' in food.

The sense of smell is far more perceptive than the sense of taste. Our noses can distinguish between several thousand different volatile compounds – quite a contrast with the five basic flavours. You might be surprised to hear it, but most of what we need to know about a wine is filtered through the nasal passages. Your first inclination might be to pour a wine straight down your throat, but by doing so you are depriving yourself of a good deal of its complexity and enjoyment. If you watch a great taster in action, it's her nose rather than palate that does most of the work. This is even truer of whisky blenders, who rarely taste the liquid in question.

Our noses have two functions, smell (called 'orthonasal olfaction') and 'retronasal olfaction'. The first occurs when we sniff a glass of wine and identify smells of grapefruits, sweaty leather saddles or what have you. The second, often confused with the sense of taste, takes place when we roll a wine across our palates and down our throats. As we do so, some odours are released into the nasal cavity by the back door, hence the term 'retronasal'. When we taste wine, we are also smelling it.

The good news for men is that there is no sign, as yet, that women are born with a superior sense of smell, although the senses of taste and smell may overlap to a certain degree. In theory at least, men can learn to smell – if not strictly speaking taste – as well as women. 'Taste is hard-wired,' says Professor Bartoshuk, 'but smell is learnt. That said, women are often better at describing smells, if not necessarily at detecting them.'

Jilly Goolden, who made her name with extravagant tasting terms such as 'absolute mangoes' and 'the thud of the cheesy foot' as a wine expert on the BBC's Food and Drink programme, agrees that 'women are more alert to most smells than men'. She also thinks that women are less inhibited when it comes to expressing themselves. 'Women aren't afraid of being told they're wrong, because they have this insurrectional quality. They don't carry as much baggage as men do; they've got less to lose.' Goolden says that professional female wine tasters aren't necessarily more skilled than their male counterparts, but that 'if you compare a man and a woman in the street, the woman would win hands down every time. It's not necessarily a reflection of tasting superiority, but there is a definite difference between women and blokes.'

There are a number of possible reasons for this. Women tend to be more accustomed to using food-related vocabulary. They also do most of the cooking and shopping. Jane Hunt, a Master of Wine, says that nurture and conditioning have a lot to do with women's greater interest in smells. 'Perfume, clean hair and cosmetics are things little girls grow up with. Little boys don't notice things in the same way. You've only got to walk into the changing room of a boys' school to appreciate this.'

Women may wash more often, spend more on perfume, learn to describe smells at a younger age and be better at identifying PTU on blotting paper, but does this make them better wine tasters? Call me a chauvinist, but I think that, for most people, getting better at wine tasting has more to do with application and experience than gender. There are genuinely gifted tasters out there – Oz Clarke is one of them – but for most of us, male or female, learning how to taste is all about time and effort. Women may have more advantages, be they the result of nature or nurture, but neither sex has a monopoly on hard graft.

POULTRY

Indonesian-style Chicken with Vegetables

Ken Hom

This is a typically hearty, family-style stir-fry that I have encountered numerous times in Jakarta. Indonesian cooks do not marinate their meat in the Chinese manner, with soy sauce, rice wine, etc. However, they often stir-fry it with pungent, aromatic ingredients such as shrimp paste and chilli peppers. The results are just as tasty, and a perfect informal supper for a large crowd.

Serves 4-6 • preparation 35 minutes

225g (8oz) (1 head) broccoli
225g (8oz) asparagus
225g (8oz) (1 cup) baby sweetcorn
3 tbsp groundnut (peanut) oil
450g (1lb) boneless, skinless chicken thighs, cut into 2.5cm (1 inch) pieces
2 tbsp finely sliced garlic
3 tbsp finely sliced shallots
2 large, fresh red chilli peppers, deseeded and sliced
1 tbsp finely sliced fresh root ginger
1½ tbsp light soy sauce
2 tsp shrimp paste
2 tsp sugar
1 tsp salt
225g (8oz) (1 cup) button mushrooms, thinly sliced
2 tbsp chicken stock or water
freshly ground pepper

Cut the stalks off the broccoli and divide the heads into small florets. Peel the stalks and thinly slice them on the diagonal. Trim the woody ends off the asparagus and then cut into 4 cm (1½ inch) lengths.

Blanch the broccoli and baby sweetcorn in a large pan of boiling salted water for 3 minutes. Drain, and plunge them into cold water to stop them cooking further, then drain again.

Heat a wok or large frying pan over a high heat. Add the oil and, when it is very hot and slightly smoking, add the chicken pieces and stir-fry for 5 minutes or until golden brown. Remove the chicken with a slotted spoon and leave to drain in a colander or sieve.

Reheat the wok over a high heat until it is medium hot. Add the garlic, shallots, chilli peppers and ginger and stir-fry for about 2 minutes, until golden brown. Then add the soy sauce, shrimp paste, sugar, salt and pepper and stir-fry for 1 minute.

Now add the broccoli, corn, asparagus and mushrooms and continue to stir-fry for 3 minutes.

Return the drained chicken to the wok, add the stock or water and cook over a high heat for 5 minutes or until the chicken is thoroughly cooked. Turn out on to a platter and serve at once.

Taken from *Ken Hom's Top100 Stir-Fry Recipes.*

Succulent Creamy Chicken Tikka

(Murgh Malai Tikka)

Anjum Anand

This chicken tikka is milder and smoother than the traditional dish that is synonymous with Indian food, in both spiciness and heat. Normally these kebabs would be marinated in cream and nuts. I have retained the nuts, which contain a healthy fat, but have left out the cream; the dish is still delicious without it. You can serve it as an appetizer, snack, a sandwich filling or for a main course. It can be cooked either on a grill or barbecue, or baked in the oven.

Serves 2 as a main course or 4 as appetizers (quantities can be doubled)

2 chicken breasts, skinned, boned and cubed
vegetable oil to brush the grill or baking tray
lemon juice to taste
½ tsp garam masala
sliced raw red onions, lemon wedges and fresh coriander to garnish

Marinade

75ml (2½fl oz) low-fat yoghurt, beaten
2 tsp mustard or vegetable oil
scant ½ tsp each turmeric, red chilli and dried mango powders
½ tsp garam masala
1 tsp dried fenugreek leaves, crumbled
2 good pinches each of carom, fennel and green cardamom seeds and black peppercorns (ground together)
2 tsp each garlic and ginger pastes
1 tbsp cashew nuts, soaked in water for 30 minutes and made into a paste in a pestle and mortar
1 rounded tbsp gram flour (besam)
1 egg yolk
½ tsp salt or to taste

Whisk together the ingredients for the marinade and tip into a plastic bag or non-metallic bowl. Taste for salt and chilli, and adjust if necessary. Pierce the chicken all over, add to the marinade and stir to coat properly. Marinate for as long as possible, preferably overnight, in the fridge. Bring back to room temperature and discard the marinade.

continued overleaf

Preheat the oven to 200°C / 400°F / Gas Mark 6. Alternatively preheat the grill and brush the rack with oil. Thread the chicken pieces on to soaked wooden or metal skewers and grill until done, about 6-8 minutes, turning every 2-3 minutes; or bake on the top shelf of the preheated oven on an oiled baking tray and cook until done, about 6 - 8 minutes, turning halfway though cooking and basting with extra oil. The chicken should be slightly charred at the edges.

Using a fork, slide the chicken pieces off the skewers. Squeeze the lemon juice, sprinkle with the garam masala and serve hot with the garnishes.

Taken from *Indian Every Day, Light, Healthy Indian Food* By Anjum Anand. Published by Headline 2003

Photo: Siân Irvine

Koluu

Spiced and Glazed Chicken Barefoot Style

4 breasts of chicken
2 onions (sliced)
salt/pepper
juice of ½ lemon
1 tsp curry powder

For the Glaze
1 tbsp white vinegar
3 tbsp mango chutney
3 tbsp red currant jelly
60g / 2oz seedless raisins
1 tbsp honey
1 tbsp chopped coriander leaves

Place the sliced onions in a roasting pan. In a bowl season the chicken breasts with salt, pepper, curry powder and lemon juice. Place the chicken on top of the sliced onions. Roast in moderate oven (180°C or Gas Mark 4) for 15 minutes.

Place all the glaze ingredients in a pan and heat gently on a low fire until ingredients are well blended.

After the chicken has been in the oven for 15 minutes, spoon a little of the glaze and continue to roast for a further 20 minutes, basting occasionally with the glaze.

When done, remove chicken breasts from the roasting pan and spread remaining glaze.

This chicken dish is ideal to be served with steamed or buttered rice.

Photo: Asanga Dissanayake

Atul Kochhar

Butter Chicken

(Chicken in spicy tomato and onion sauce)

British "chicken tikka masala" was probably inspired from this Indian classic. This is a favourite recipe among North Indians. I use tandoori chicken for this recipe for enhanced flavours, but you may use plain chicken or buy in ready made tandoori chicken from your local Indian. If you wish to use plain chicken, sauté it lightly in 1 tbsp oil to seal and then cook in sauce.

Serves 4

1 whole tandoori chicken, cut into 8 pieces
2 tbsp vegetable oil
2 tbsp roughly chopped ginger
1kg tomatoes, roughly chopped
2 tbsp butter
1 medium onion, finely sliced
1 green chilli, slit from tip to tail
1 tsp fenugreek leaf powder
1 tsp garam masala powder
1 tsp red chilli powder
2 tbsp honey
1 tsp salt
2 tbsp finely chopped coriander leaves
4 tbsp fresh single cream

In a heavy bottom pan heat vegetable oil, ginger, tomatoes & 100ml water and cook on slow heat for 35-40 minutes until tomatoes melt to form a sauce. Blend to a smooth sauce and strain through fine sieve and hold until required.

In another pan, heat butter and sauté onions for 3 minutes until a light brown colour. Add slit green chillies, and add tomato sauce. Simmer and add remaining ingredients except cream and coriander leaves. Cook the sauce for 30 minutes to allow the spices to blend with sauce, then add cream and simmer for 3-5 minutes.

Add chicken pieces and cook for further 10-15 minutes until chicken is well cooked and well heated. Sprinkle chopped coriander and serve with pulao.

Braised Turkey with Chillies, Coconut and Lemon Grass

Turkey thighs are relatively inexpensive. The dark meat has a richer flavour than the lighter breast meat - and it is a perfect match for the distinctive flavours of Thai cooking.

Serves 4

2 turkey thighs, boned, rolled and tied (ask your butcher to do this)
4 fat garlic cloves, 2 cut into slivers and 2 finely chopped
A handful of fresh coriander
25g unsalted butter
3 hot red chillies, deseeded and finely sliced, not ringed
1 onion, freshly chopped
250ml white wine
250ml turkey or chicken stock
2 stalks of lemon grass
400ml canned coconut milk
sea salt and freshly ground mixed peppercorns

Using a sharp knife, make small incisions in the turkey rolls and insert the garlic slivers and coriander.

Melt the butter in a heavy-based frying pan until foaming, then add the turkey and sear until golden on all sides. Remove and put into a casserole.

Add the onion, chopped garlic and chillies to the same frying pan and cook until softened. Transfer to the casserole. Pour the wine into the pan, bring to the boil and cool until reduced by half. Add the stock and return to the boil.

Remove and discard the outer layer of the lemon grass then crush the stems with a rolling pin or heavy knife to release flavour. Add to the pan.

Add the coconut milk, return to the boil and season. Pour over the turkey and vegetables, cook uncovered in a pre-heated oven at 200°C (400°F) Gas Mark 6 for about 20 minutes. Cover, reduce to 180°C. (350°F) Gas Mark 4 and cook for a further 1hr 30 mins or until tender. For the last 15 minutes of cooking, remove the lid and increase the temperature to 200°C (400°F) Gas Mark 6 to brown the turkey.

Slice the turkey and serve with the sauce, Thai fragrant rice and coriander.

Tessa Bramley

Tessa Bramley is the chef/owner of the Old Vicarage Restaurant in the village of Ridgeway, near Sheffield. She is a senior Fellow of the Master Chefs of Great Britain and holder of a coveted Michelin star. She has presented TV shows for the BBC, Channel 4 and ITV and writes a regular food column for the Yorkshire Post.
She has published six books. Her two latest titles are: *Casseroles – Comfort Food at its Best* and *Perfect Puddings* published by Ryland Peters & Small

Ed Baines

Baines is the chef and co-owner of Randall & Aubin, the champagne and oyster bars in Soho and the Fulham Road, the Ifield in Chelsea and the Belsize in Belsize Park. He worked for Anton Mosimann at the Dorchester and then spent some years cooking on one of the world's most exclusive yachts, at hotels in Juan-les-Pins and Queensland and then back home in London at Bibendum, River Café and Daphne's. His first TV series *Lunch* with Ed Baines had him cooking for, and then lunching with, his famous friends. *Ed Baines Entertains* is also broadcast in the ITV Carlton region. He is co-presenter of *Good Food Live* for the UK Food channel and is a regular on *Saturday Kitchen* (BBC2). Kyle Cathie published his first book, *Entertain*, in 2001.

Crispy Duck Teriyaki Noodle Salad

Serves 4

2 whole free-range duck breasts
2 tbsp teriyaki sauce
2 bunches of fine rice noodles (glass noodles)
100g (4oz) extra-fine green beans
20 sprigs of fresh coriander, plus more to garnish
2 banana shallots, thinly sliced
4 spring onions, thinly sliced

For the oriental teriyaki dressing

8 tbsp teriyaki sauce
4 tbsp soy sauce
6 tbsp sesame oil
2 tsp clear honey
juice of 2 limes
4 garlic cloves, thinly sliced
2.5cm (1inch) piece of root ginger, grated

Preheat the oven to 200°C/400°F/Gas Mark 6. Make the dressing: mix all the liquid ingredients together, then add the sliced garlic and grated ginger. Lightly score the duck fat and spoon one-third of the dressing over the duck.

Place a dry flameproof baking dish on the hob over a medium heat and seal the duck breasts, fat side first, then place the baking dish in the oven and cook for 8 minutes. Remove from the oven and allow to cool. Keep the oven on.

Once the duck is cool enough to handle, slice each breast into thin slices and then toss the slices in 2 more tablespoons of the teriyaki dressing. Put them back in the oven for a further 2 minutes to allow the dressing to caramelize slightly (a bit like sweet-and-sour pork).

Soak the noodles as per the instructions on the packet. Bring a saucepan of water to the boil and blanch the beans for 1 minute. Drain and add to the cooked noodles, then mix in the coriander sprigs, shallots and spring onions. Add the slices of duck with the remaining dressing and mix well. Garnish with some more coriander and serve.

Taken from *Entertain* by Ed Baines. Published by Kyle Cathie 2001.

Notes

Notes

Jancis Robinson

Jancis Robinson OBE, Master of Wine and award-winning TV host, has written millions of words about wine, in books such as *The Oxford Companion to Wine* and the latest, 5th, edition of *The World Atlas of Wine* (with Hugh Johnson), as wine correspondent of the *Financial Times*, and for www.jancisrobinson.com, nowadays her principal preoccupation.

New Latitude Wines

Frank Norel is a wine writer based in Thailand. For a talk he gave late last year at a conference in Bangkok on the expanding world of wine he coined a phrase which I suspect will become increasingly familiar to us: New Latitude Wines.

As someone who updated the classic of wine geography *The World Atlas of Wine* less than three years ago, I am fully aware of how the conventional map of the wine world looks. For years we have drawn two bands around the globe, roughly between latitudes 30 and 50, to denote those parts of it deemed suitable for viticulture.

But all this is changing fast, and not just because global warming has given new hope to those growing vines at high latitudes – the likes of my countrymen trying to ripen grapes in the English countryside, their counterparts in Holland, Denmark and Poland, and the man who is currently planting vines 950 kilometers south of Santiago de Chile.

Advances in refrigeration and irrigation techniques, not to mention much greater control over how and when vines grow, have opened up to the grapevine vast tracts of the world previously thought unsuitable for viticulture.

This was brought home to me forcibly during my first visit to Brazil last November. On my first night in Sao Paulo I was subjected to a heavy sales pitch for, and tasting of, a new wine from the San Francisco Valley in the far north of Brazil near Recife grown just eight or nine degrees south of the equator. This deep red wine, the result of a partnership between the wine distributor Expand, some local growers and the Portuguese wine producer Dao Sul, is based on Syrah and Cabernet grapes grown on pergolas in desert conditions alongside many other fruits watered from the nearby San Francisco river.

The result, as far as my jetlagged palate could tell, is a perfectly respectable, deliberately modern, mass market red. It is being targeted at the British supermarkets, probably to be called Rio Red. (A wine called simply 'River' would not work for Portuguese or Spanish speakers, but the word Rio has exotic and definitely Brazilian connotations for us British.)

Just a few days later, at a tasting organised of some of Brazil's best wines (it will be some time before they present a serious challenge to Châteaux Lafite and Latour) I came across another red from this subequatorial area, Terranova Shiraz (sic) 2002 from one of Brazil's best-known producers Miolo - another perfectly acceptable, ultra-modern, flashy red produced from yields reportedly about six tonnes per acre (more than 100 hl/ha).

What's so attractive to producers about these tropical wines of course is that the vine is completely subservient to man. Thanks to careful timing of irrigation, pruning and application of crop regulators in the form of special hormones, they can choose how often the plants will produce a crop. In the San Francisco Valley the producers seem to agree that more than two crops a year is too greedy and weakens the vine uneconomically early in its life. But even two crops a year of course halves (already low) production costs at a stroke.

Plant scientists today are convinced that all plants, not just the vine, are very much more 'plastic' than was previously thought. Put them in a new environment and they will respond with remarkable speed and efficiency. They have no choice after all. Unlike animals, they cannot move. An Indian-born Cambridge scientist told me recently with pride how successfully she was growing plants native to some of the hottest parts of her native land outdoors in Cambridge, one of England's most notoriously chilly towns. Plants quite naturally adopt coping mechanisms in changed environments.

The official plant science line is that a vine producing two or more crops a year may not express winter dormancy but it will almost certainly exhibit some other, possibly useful, characteristic in its stead. We already know, for example, that drought stress results in an impressive build-up of both anthocyanins and sugars - which helps to explain the deep colour and respectable alcohol levels of those two Brazilian reds.

In Thailand, the country that inspired the term New Latitude Wines, there are now no fewer than five wineries turning grapes into wine. One of the most ambitious, and one that uses exclusively Thai-grown grapes, is the Siam Winery, founded as recently as 1996 by the man who invented the energy drink Red Bull, Khun Chalerm Yoovidya. Perhaps to atone for inflicting Red Bull on the world's nervous systems, he is now trying to develop Thailand's wine culture.

The grapes, Malaga Blanc for white wines and the local dark-skinned Pok Dum with Shiraz and Black Muscat, are bought from farmers in the Chao Prayha Delta, an hour south west of Bangkok, where the vineyards effectively float on the river water. Plantings have apparently increased from 8,000 to 12,000 acres of floating vines since 1996 and, while the name they have chosen for their international brand, Monsoon Valley, is not guaranteed to inspire traditional wine lovers with confidence, they are very clear in their objective of promoting the wines specifically to partner Thai food in restaurants around the world. They are also developing experimental vineyards further north on higher ground in the Tap Gwang District, near Khao Yai, which is also the name of the wine subsidiary of the brewers of Thailand's leading beer Singha. The historic Chinese wine company Changyu recently announced it is planning a joint venture winery with its Thai importers, while Chateau de Loei has been producing red and white table wines in north east Thailand for a decade now. The latitude range of all these Thai vineyards is well under 18 degrees north of the equator.

Now that wine is such a popular interest in so many parts of the world, vineyards are springing up at equally low latitudes in such unlikely places as Vietnam, southern India, Indonesia, Ethiopia, Kenya, Bolivia, Peru and doubtless several other countries currently harbouring an embryonic wine industry unknown to me.

I still find it hard to believe that New Latitude Wines will ever be seriously good, but then that's what was said about New World Wines not that long ago.

Taken from www.jancisrobinson.com 2004

MEAT

Eddy Pratomo

CHARGÉ D'AFFAIRES,
EMBASSY OF THE
REPUBLIC OF INDONESIA,
LONDON

Eddy Pratomo was born in Semarang, Indonesia in 1953. He started his career in the Foreign Ministry in 1982 having obtained a degree in civil law. International postings have included working with the United Nations in New York and as Head of Political Affairs Department in Geneva. At the beginning of May 2004, he started his posting as the Deputy Chief of Mission and Chargé d'Affaires of the Embassy of the Republic of Indonesia in London. Mr Eddy Pratomo is married with two daughters and a son.

Rendang

(Rendang is a traditional West Sumatra beef dish)

As it takes so long to cook, and keeps for a long time, it is worth making a large quantity.

1½kg (3½lb) brisket or top side beef
6 shallots
3 cloves garlic
salt
1 tsp ground ginger
1 tsp turmeric
3 fresh red chillies
1 cube of fresh laos (galangal)
7½ cups (3 pints) coconut milk
1 fresh salam leaf (bay-leaf)
Fresh kunyit leaf (turmeric leaf) optional

Cut the meat into biggish cubes. Crush the shallots and garlic with some salt; add ginger; turmeric; chilli and galangal. Mix them and put into the coconut milk. Add the meat and the various leaves. Cook in a wok, letting mixture bubble gently and stirring it occasionally until it becomes very thick. This should take 1½ to 2 hours. Taste and add salt if necessary.

When the mixture is thick, the slow cooking must continue, but now the meat and sauce must be stirred continuously until all the sauce has been absorbed into the meat and the meat itself has become a golden brown. This will take at least half an hour. Serve the rendang with plain boiled rice. The Rendang will keep for many days in a deep-freezer.

Empal Gentong

(Braised beef brisket, beef ribs and beef tongue soup)

A 'gentong' in Indonesia is a cooking pot used mainly to prepare the 'jamu' or traditional medicine. This recipe originates from Cirebon, a sea-side city 200km east of Jakarta. With its unique, rich flavours this is probably one of my top Indonesian dishes.

Selamat makan!

Preparation 45 minutes • cooking 2 hours

Ingredients for the *Empal Gentong*

500g beef ribs, cut in small pieces, bone in
8 slices beef tongue blanched, skin removed, cooked and cut in 1cm slices
700g beef brisket, quite lean
¼-½ hard coconut, grated finely
3 salam leaves, (or small bay leaves)
3cm fresh galangal, peeled and crushed
4 lime leaves, fresh
3 sticks lemon grass, peeled and crushed
3cm fresh ginger
6 cloves
1 cinnamon stick, 4cm
3 cardamom pods, seeds removed

continued overleaf

Antoine Audran

Born in France 45 years ago and after many years roaming the world and working as executive chef in some top hotels and restaurants around the world, I decided 3 years ago to launch my own business in Jakarta, Indonesia. We opened the French restaurant named Java Bleu in south Jakarta, a small but very successful outlet which focuses on top quality products and customer recognition. Our next stage, which will be effective in July 2005, is the launching of an industrial kitchen which will focus on food processing and catering using some modern and efficient culinary production techniques.

Mixed Spice Paste

16 small shallots, peeled and sliced
8 cloves garlic, peeled, end removed, crushed
12 kemiri nuts, roasted and chopped
(can substitute macadamias)
1 tsp coriander seeds
½ tsp white pepper corns
6cm cumin root, sliced
salt, to taste
20ml oil for frying, corn oil is best

Serve with

Steamed rice, enough for 8 (roughly
enough, dry, to fill a 20fl oz jug)
2 tbsp chives, finely chopped
4 tbsp spring onions, roughly chopped
40g shallots, sliced and deep fried
8 cloves garlic, sliced and fried
Melinjo crackers (or beef skin
crackers)
Chili sauce
Red and birds'eye chillies, finely
sliced
Sweet soy sauce

Dry fry the grated coconut flesh to a golden colour, reserve

In a large cooking pot, place the beef ribs and brisket, salam leaves, galangal, lime leaves, lemon grass, ginger, cloves, cinnamon, cardamom and a little salt. Pour in 2 litres of cold water. Bring slowly to the boil and simmer over a low heat until the beef brisket is fully cooked and tender.

Remove the brisket from the broth, slice it and reserve.

When the ribs are tender, remove and reserve also.

For the spice paste, (which can be prepared in advance) use a pestle and mortar to crush and mash all the ingredients until they reach a smooth consistency. Now heat the oil in a small steel wok and gently fry the spice paste until all the flavours are extracted.

Add the beef broth to the spice paste and cook over a medium heat for ten minutes. Now add back the beef brisket and ribs. Also add the beef tongue and the coconut and heat through gently. Add more water if the soup is too thick.

Correct the seasoning with more salt and white pepper if necessary. Sprinkle on top the chives, spring onions and fried shallot and garlic slices. Serve at once with the warm rice, crackers, chillies and sauces

Anthony Morrison

Born in Sydney Australia, Anthony Morrison developed an early love for food and creating new dishes through working in his family's catering business while still at school. Before coming to London in 1997 Anthony worked in some of Australia's top restaurants, hotels and resorts in Sydney, the Hunter Valley wine region and on The Great Barrier Reef. Since coming to London, Anthony has worked for the Conran group, culminating in running the kitchens at Conran's Soho flagship Mezzo and since 2002 has been the Executive Head Chef for The Rock Garden group overseeing the Rock Garden restaurant, the International and Fire & Stone which is due to open this year. Anthony has developed a style of cuisine that takes in influences from many different Asian and South Pacific countries as well as the best that Europe has to offer.

Black Peppered Beef Hotpot

This dish can be served in any type of bowl but for best results a clay hot pot should be used. These pots are readily available from Asian grocery stores.

Stock

250ml good chicken stock
20g ginger finely chopped
2 garlic cloves crushed
1 red chilli sliced
2 spring onions sliced
4 dried shiitake mushrooms (soaked)
30ml light soya sauce
30ml sake
20g yellow rock sugar

Saute ginger, garlic, spring onion and chilli until soft.

Add the chicken stock and mushrooms and simmer for 15 minutes.

Remove from the stove and add the soya sauce, sake and rock sugar and stir until sugar is dissolved. Leave the stock to cool and then strain the liquid. Adjust the seasoning using light soya sauce.

Beef and vegetables

300g finely sliced beef filet tossed in lots of freshly ground black pepper
2 Blanched and sliced bok choy
10 Blanched and sliced baby corn
8 blanched and sliced asparagus spears
2 spring onions finely sliced
1 chilli finely sliced and de-seeded

Place the clay pot in the oven to heat up.

Warm the stock in a saucepan and add the blanched vegetables

Heat a heavy frying pan with a little vegetable oil until very hot and the oil is starting to smoke.

Quickly sear the beef so as to add as much colour to the meat as possible but not to over cook it.

Place the seared beef into the hot clay pot.

Pour in the hot stock and vegetables.

Place the sliced chilli and spring onions over the top of the dish.

Cover with the hot pot lid and serve to the table immediately.

This dish should be accompanied by steamed fragrant jasmine rice.

Paul Gayler

Asian-style Steak au Poivre

This take on the classic French peppered steak is inspired by my love of oriental food. The vegetables should remain crisp, the steak peppery, with a slightly sweet sauce.

Serves 4

1 tbsp black peppercorns, coarsely cracked
1 tbsp Szechuan peppercorns, cracked
4 x 175g (6oz) fillet steaks
4 tbsp vegetable oil
2 tbsp cognac
4 tbsp mirin (Japanese sweet rice wine)
1 tbsp corn syrup or honey
2.5cm (1in) piece of fresh root ginger, grated
600ml (1 pint) well-flavoured chicken stock
4 tbsp light soy sauce
1 tbsp ketjap manis (Indonesian soy sauce)
2 tsp arrowroot, mixed with 2 tsp cold water
25g (1oz) unsalted butter, diced
Salt

For the vegetables
3 tbsp sesame oil
1 garlic clove, crushed
1cm (½in) piece of fresh root ginger, thinly shredded
4 small pak choi, separated into leaves
1 carrot, sliced
8 spring onions, halved
100g (4oz) shiitake mushrooms, thickly sliced
2 red radishes, sliced
50g (2oz) beansprouts

Mix the cracked peppercorns together and then, using the heel of your hand, press them evenly over one side of each steak. Leave for 30 minutes.

continued overleaf

Heat the oil in a large, heavy-based frying pan until smoking. Season the steaks with salt, then add them to the pan, pepper-side down. Fry over a moderate heat, turning once, for 3–4 minutes for medium-rare, longer if you prefer your meat more cooked. Remove from the pan and keep warm.

Spoon off any fat from the pan, then return it to the heat, add the cognac and flambé it with a match, standing well back. When the flames have died down, add the mirin, corn syrup or honey, ginger, chicken stock and soy sauces. Bring to the boil, then reduce the heat and simmer until the liquid is reduced by half its volume. Stir in the arrowroot mixture and boil for 1 minute, until thickened, then strain through a fine sieve into a clean pan. Finally whisk in the butter a piece at a time. Keep warm while you prepare the vegetables.

For the vegetables, heat the sesame oil in a wok or large frying pan, add the garlic and ginger and leave to infuse for 10 seconds. Add the vegetables, stir-fry for 3–4 minutes, then season. Arrange on 4 serving plates, place the fillet steak on top and pour the sauce over.

HOT TIP

This recipe is also very good made with a meaty fish such as monkfish or turbot.

Burmese Style Pork

Keith Floyd

Serves 4-6

1½kg Pork, cubed
1 Red Onion, Peeled
12 Garlic Cloves, Peeled
1cm / ½ Inch Piece Fresh Ginger Peeled
2 tbsp White Wine Vinegar
1 tbsp Sesame Oil
3 tbsp Peanut Oil
2 Fresh Red Chillies Finely Chopped
1 tsp Turmeric Powder
1 tsp Shrimp Paste

Put the onion, garlic, ginger, shallots and vinegar into a food processor and whiz together. Transfer to a bowl and mix in the pork. Leave to marinate in the fridge for about 2 hours.

When the pork has marinated, take out the meat, reserving the marinade. Heat the sesame oil and 2 tablespoons of the peanut oil in a large pan and fry the pork, turning until lightly golden all over. Cover with water, bring to the boil and simmer for about 1½ hours.

In another pan, heat the remaining peanut oil, add the marinade mixture and the chillies and fry for 4-5 minutes. Add the turmeric and shrimp paste and fry for a couple more minutes.

Add this to the pork mixture, stirring well and simmer for a further 10 minutes.

Photo: Con Poulos

Chilli Jam Beef Stir-fry

Serves 4

6 large mild red chillies, seeds removed
1 tbsp roughly chopped ginger
1 onion, quartered
3 tsp shrimp paste
⅓ cup brown sugar
2 tbsp vegetable oil
650g (21oz) beef strips
4 green onions (scallions), sliced
200g (7oz) green beans, trimmed

Place the chillies, ginger, onion, shrimp paste, sugar and oil in a food processor and process until finely chopped. Heat a non-stick frying pan over medium-high heat and add the chilli paste. Cook, stirring, for 5-7 minutes or until the mixture is thick and fragrant. Add the beef to the pan and stir-fry for 3 minutes. Add the green onions and beans, cover and cook for a further 3 minutes or until the vegetables are tender. Serve with steamed jasmine rice.

Taken from *The Instant Cook* published by Harper Collins 2004

Donna Hay

Donna Hay is Australia's best-known name in cookbook and magazine publishing. Her recipes are renowned for their fresh modern flavours, stylish presentation and ease of preparation. Donna's relaxed approach and contemporary style have become a benchmark for cookbooks and recipe writing, witnessed in eight phenomenally successful books including *Off The Shelf*, *Modern Classics Book 1* and *Book 2*, and her latest, *The Instant Cook*. Donna Hay is also known for her popular weekly columns in newspapers around Australia and New Zealand and in the *New York Post*. The bi-monthly *Donna Hay Magazine* is available at selected stockists in the US, Canada and UK.

Gary Rhodes

Gary Rhodes, Chef, restaurateur, celebrity and author; his distinguished career and history of stunning restaurants has won him a constellation of Michelin stars. New ventures include the launch of a range of bespoke condiments and Kids in the Kitchen children's cooking packs, designed to encourage a younger generation of cooks. Last year Gary opened his London restaurant, Rhodes Twenty Four, with spectacular views over the City from Tower 42. Gary began experimenting in the kitchen as a teenager, preparing family meals while his mother was at work. His first major culinary achievement, at the age of 13, was a Sunday roast followed by a classic British dessert – Marguerite Patten's steamed lemon sponge pudding. One look at his family's delighted faces as they got stuck in was enough to convince him that a cook's life was the one for him.

Oriental Style Sticky Lamb Chops

Serves 4

8 chump lamb chops
320g (11oz) jar plum sauce
4 tsp clear honey
4 tsp dark soy sauce
2 garlic cloves, crushed
2.5cm (1inch) ginger, chopped
2 spring onions, cut into 2.5cm long pieces
2 red chillies, finely chopped

250g (9oz) packet egg noodles
1 tbsp sesame oil
3 spring onions for curling
227g (8oz) can water chestnuts, drained and roughly chopped
227g (8oz) can bamboo shoots, drained
1 red chilli, finely sliced

Pre heat the oven to 220°C/425°F/Gas 7

Mix half the plum sauce with the honey, soy sauce, garlic, ginger, spring onions and half the chopped chillies

Place the chops in a roasting tin and coat with the sauce. Marinate for 3-4 minutes.

Roast in the oven for 12-15 minutes, turning once.

Drop the noodles into boiling water and cook until tender. Then toss them in sesame oil with spring onion curls, water chestnuts and bamboo shoots.

Serve the lamb on the noodles with the sauce spooned over the top. Garnish with chilli slices.

Note: To make spring onion curls, soak shredded spring onions in iced water.

Taken from *Great Fast Food* published by Ebury Press 2000

Shanth Fernando

Marinated Lamb Cutlets with Yellow Rice and Rocket

Serves 2

1 cup basmati rice
1 tsp butter
1 tbsp finely chopped onions
¼ tsp turmeric
1 cardamom seed - bruised
2 cloves
1 stick cinnamon
chicken stock
toasted slivered almonds for garnish
1 small bunch rocket

4 lamb cutlets

Marinade
1 tbsp curry powder
¼ tsp chilli flakes
2 garlic cloves, chopped
2 tbsp olive oil
a good pinch of sea salt and freshly ground black pepper

Place all the ingredients for the marinade in a bowl, stir and combine. Place the lamb cutlets in the marinade and toss to combine. Cover with plastic wrap and place in the refrigerator for two hours. Bring to room temperature before cooking.

Fry chopped onions in butter in a large saucepan until golden brown. Add washed and drained basmati rice, bruised cardamom seed, cinnamon stick, cloves and turmeric and stir for a few seconds. Add sufficient chicken stock to boil rice.

Heat frying pan over high heat for a minute, add lamb cutlets and cook for one minute for medium rare.

Remove cutlets from the pan and stir fry the chopped rocket leaves in the jus for one minute.

Serve two lamb cutlets to a plate on the rice and top with rocket and slivered almonds.

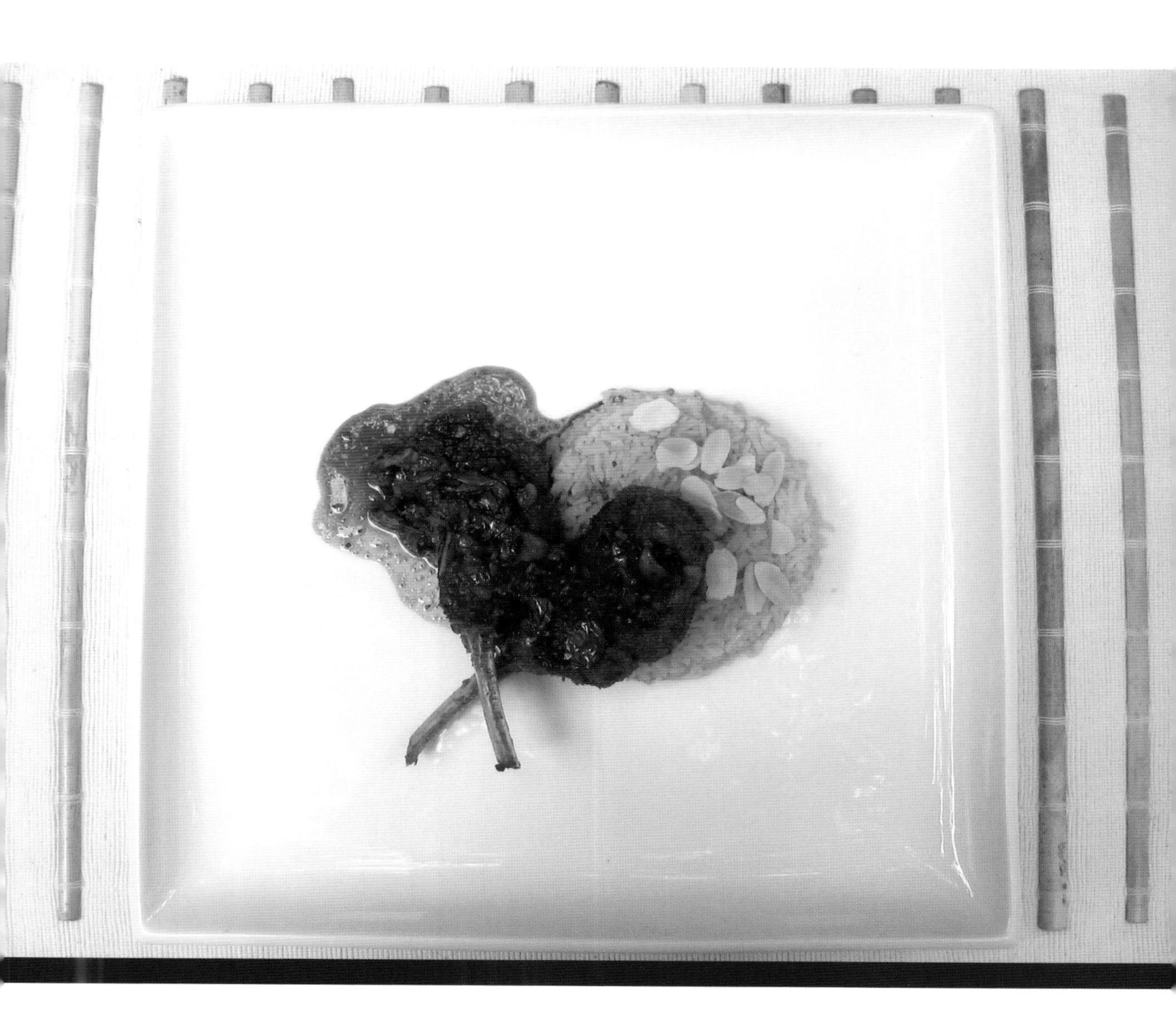

Nua-Look-Gaa-Pad-Bai-Salani

Thai Lamb Stir-fried with Mint

Pat Chapman

I encountered a recipe similar to this at the seaside restaurant Gypsy World which nestles in the coconut palms of Phuket's Siray (Ko-Sire) Island. Known for its Buddha surveying the scene in recline on its hilltop, and its sea gypsy village and sea food, it was an unlikely place to find lamb, which is mostly only eaten by Thai Moslems. This recipe calls for coconut. When the chef calls for it, assistants simply pluck them from the trees.

Serves 4

700g lean leg of lamb, weighed after stage 1
4 tbsp sunflower or soy oil
5cm cube ginger or galangale shredded
50g tinned sliced bamboo shoot
200ml thick coconut milk
6 or 7 spring onion, bulbs and leaves, cross cut
1 or more green chillies, shredded
4 tbsp freshly squeezed lime juice
1 tsp fish sauce (nam pla)
1 tsp light soy sauce
6 tbsp chopped fresh mint leaves

Garnish

some fried cashew nuts
red chilli tassels
fried garlic

Divest the lamb of any unwanted matter. Cut it into thin strips about 4cm x 2cm x 4mm each.

Heat the oil in your wok. Briskly stir-fry the lamb strips for about 4 to 5 minutes.

Add the ginger and bamboo shoots and enough of their liquid to stop the sizzling.

Stir-fry for another couple of minutes then add the remaining ingredients.

When simmering, garnish and serve.

Hugh Fearnley-Whittingstall

Hugh Fearnley-Whittingstall is widely known as a writer, broadcaster and campaigner for his uncompromising commitment to real food. His series for Channel 4 – most recently *Beyond River Cottage* – have earned him a huge popular following. *Beyond River Cottage* saw the transformation of some seriously mucky cow barns into River Cottage HQ, where Hugh and the RCHQ team now run a number of events and courses designed to promote their 'grow your own' philosophy and provide an environment where people can discuss, eat and learn about the very best home-grown, local, and seasonal food. Hugh lives in Dorset with Marie and their sons Oscar and Freddie. He is Patron of the National Farmers' Retail and Markets Association (FARMA).

Chinese-style Spare Ribs and Pig's Trotters

Serves 6, or more as part of a bigger Chinese spread

4 pig's trotters
500g spare ribs of pork, in short lengths of 2-4 rib width
2 tbsp sunflower oil
5cm piece of fresh ginger root, grated
4 large garlic cloves, finely crushed
50ml dark soy sauce
100ml light soy sauce
50g light brown sugar
100ml brown rice vinegar, or cider vinegar
150ml pineapple juice, ideally fresh (apple juice works as a back-up)
Salt

This is the third book in which I have included a version of this recipe, and I keep honing and improving it. I make no apologies for labouring the point, as it's the surest way I know of converting doubters to the joys of pig's trotters – though serious doubters could use only spare ribs, doubling the quantities. Thanks again to Rose Billaud; who first showed me how to make it. Make sure that you remove all the hairs from the trotters – shave them with a razor if necessary.

Using a meat cleaver, split each pig's trotter into 4 or 6 pieces (i.e. once down the middle and once or twice across). Your butcher could do this for you.

Heat the oil in a large, heavy-based pan, add the pig's trotters and spare rib pieces and fry until browned. Add the ginger, garlic and a little salt and continue to fry to release the aromatic flavours. Add the soy sauces, sugar, vinegar, pineapple juice, and just enough water to cover. Bring to a gentle simmer, cover with a lid and leave to cook until the trotters are tender (about 2-2½ hours). Stir occasionally, and make sure the liquid is not too low.

When the trotters are cooked, remove all the meat (i.e. trotters and ribs) from the pan with a slotted spoon and put in a bowl on one side. Continue to simmer the cooking liquid gently until it has reduced to a rich, syrupy consistency. Return the meat to the pan and heat through in the sauce.

The dish can be served immediately, though all the flavour will continue to improve if it is left overnight in the refrigerator. The meat can then be eaten cold, in the jelly in which it has set, or reheated.

Serve with plain boiled rice and simple stir-fried vegetables (crunchy French beans with carrot and spring onions), or as a course in any Chinese-style banquet. Eating with the fingers has to be allowed, as does spitting out any knuckly pieces of bones from the trotters! The brave will want to eat the spare ribs bones and all.

Taken from *The River Cottage Meat Book* published by Hodder & Stoughton 2004

Photo: Simon Wheeler 2004

Sophie Grigson

Sophie is synonymous with great food, often using new and exciting ingredients in simple, easy dishes. She has a natural ability to teach cookery in an informal and friendly way, and her TV career began in 1993 with the award winning twelve part *Grow Your Greens, Eat Your Greens* for Channel 4. In 2001, Sophie won the Guild of Food Writers Cookery Journalist Award. Sophie's book, *Organic* was co-written with her husband, William Black and was published in May 2001. Sophie Grigson's *Country Kitchen* was published in September 2003 by Headline and her latest book, *The First-time Cook*, was published by Collins in 2004.

Pot Roast Pork with Star Anise, Ginger, Tamarind and Port

Pot Roast Pork with Star Anise, Ginger, Tamarind and Port. No deliberate fusion of east and west, here, just one of those kitchen coincidences of life – a bit of this and a bit of that - and a vague yen for something a little more aromatic than a straight European pot-roast. Nonetheless, the blend of soy sauce, sour tamarind and ginger with ruby port and a touch of rosemary was good enough to repeat, so I did.

Serve it western style with potatoes and spinach, or with rice and stir-fried ribbons of vegetables.

By the way, you can find ready-made tamarind puree in the spice racks in good supermarkets.

1¼-1½kg (3-3½lb) boned, rolled loin of pork
2 tbsp sunflower oil
1 onion, sliced
6 cloves garlic, whole but not peeled
2cm (¾inch) piece fresh root ginger, finely chopped
1 good sized sprig of rosemary
1 whole star anise
85ml (3fl oz) ruby port
3 tbsp dark soy sauce
1 tbsp tamarind puree, or lemon juice
2 tbsp light muscovado sugar
plenty of pepper

Wipe the pork dry with a kitchen towel. Brown all over in the oil in a heat- and oven-proof casserole. Transfer to a plate for a few minutes while you fry the onion in the same fat –not too fast at first, raising the heat slightly as it becomes tender to brown here and there. Pour off excess fat, leaving the onion behind in the dish. Now return the meat to the pan and add all the remaining ingredients. Bring up to the boil, then cover and either turn the heat down very low, or transfer to the oven, pre-heated to 140°C/275°F/Gas Mark 1.

Braise gently, turning the meat occasionally, for about 3 hours, until the meat is very tender. Skim as much fat as you can from the juices, then taste the juices and adjust seasoning. Strain and reheat if necessary. Slice the pork thickly, and drizzle with a little of the cooking juices. Serve immediately.

Taken from *Sophie Grigson's Open Kitchen* published by Hodder Headline 2003

Notes

Notes

VEGETABLES & RICE

Pat Chapman

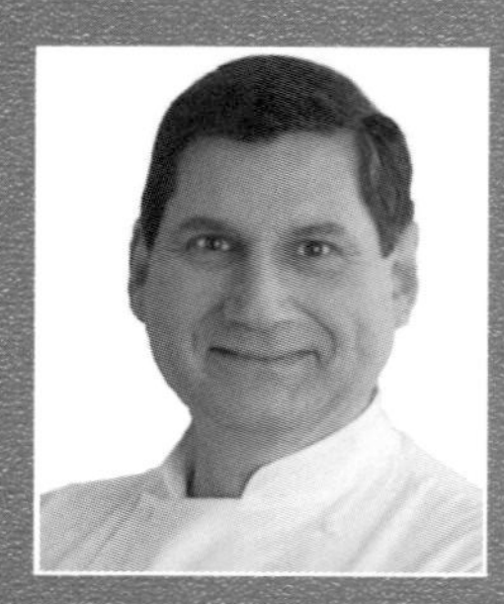

Porial Kadama

(South Indian Festival Vegetables)

At new year, India's southern-eastern state, Tamil Nadu, holds a festival called Pongal. Food is closely associated with Hindu religious festivals and the temples specialise in cooking for the masses, and dispensing it liberally to all-comers. This Porial Kadama is an example, using some interesting vegetables, and it is served with rice .

1 fennel bulb
1 kohlrabi bulb
1 celeriac bulb
15cm piece white radish (mooli)
225g red sweet potato
2 tbsp mustard blend oil
110g onions, chopped
1 tbsp split and polished urid lentils, roasted
120ml coconut milk
1 large firm mango, skinned, stoned and chopped
a few fresh pineapple chunks
2-4 fresh red chillies, chopped
1 tbsp chopped fresh coriander
salt to taste

Masala

1 tsp black mustard seeds
1 tsp cumin seeds
1 tsp sesame seeds
½ tsp turmeric
10-15 curry leaves, fresh or dried
½ tsp coriander seeds
½ tsp black cumin seeds

Peel the fennel, kohlrabi, celeriac and mooli, discarding unwanted matter. Shred them through the food processor attachment or hand grater.

Cook the potato until soft. Cut into small cubes.

Heat the oil in a karahi or wok. Stir-fry the masala for 20 seconds, then the onion for 5 minutes.

Add the coconut milk and when simmering add all the vegetables, and simmer until tender.

Add the mango, pineapple, chillies and coriander. Stir-fry until cooked to your liking adding a little water if needed, to keep things mobile.

Salt to taste and serve at once.

Eddy Pratomo

Gado-gado

(Mixed vegetable salad with peanut sauce)

This is a very popular vegetable dish, inexpensive, and very good for you. You can eat gado-gado by itself or with rice and other dishes.

Take a selection of fresh vegetables such as

3oz lettuce
3oz french beans
3oz carrots
4oz beansprout
1 quarter cucumber
2 medium size potatoes

For the garnish

1 hard boiled egg
fried shallot
prawn crackers

For the sauce

120g (4oz) peanuts
1 clove of garlic
salt
1 fresh red chilli
1 tsp brown sugar
1 cup water
1 cup coconut milk
1 tsp lemon juice
vegetable oil

First prepare the vegetables. Slice the beans and carrots. Clean the beansprouts.

Fry the peanuts in a cupful of vegetable oil for 5 to 6 minutes. Drain and let them cool. Then grind into a fine powder. Crush the chilli and garlic into a rough paste adding a little salt. Fry the paste in 1 tablespoonful of oil. Add sugar and more salt to taste; then add 1 cup of water.

Let it boil then add the ground peanuts. Add the coconut milk. Stir the mixture well and let it simmer, stirring occasionally until it becomes thick. Add the lemon juice before serving.

Boil or steam each vegetable separately for not more than 5 minutes. The beansprouts should be boiled for 2 minutes. Boil or fry the potatoes and cut into cubes.

Serve the gado-gado on a round or oval dish which is big enough to spread the vegetables out on.

Put the lettuce first and then add all the cooked vegetables and sliced boiled egg. Pour the sauce over it and garnish with fried shallots and crushed prawn crackers.

Risotto with Mushrooms and Ginger

A risotto with such distinctively Asian flavours might come as a shock if you're used to the traditional Italian recipe, but be brave and try this Oriental version. To restore the true taste of Italy to your next risotto, just leave out the ginger, substitute some Parmesan for the soy sauce and swap basil for the coriander.

Serves 4

40g (1½oz) butter
½ large onion, weighing about 150g (5oz), finely chopped
2 cloves of garlic, minced
½-1 tbsp chopped fresh ginger
750ml (1¼ pt) chicken stock
8 tbsp soy sauce (preferably Japanese)
350g (12oz) arborio or other good-quality risotto rice
2-3 spring onions, sliced
2 tbsp chopped coriander leaves (optional)

SHIITAKE MUSHROOM SAUCE
150g (5oz) shiitake mushrooms
15g (½oz) butter
2 tbsp chicken stock
2 tbsp soy sauce
1 tsp sugar

Melt 15g (½oz) of the butter in a medium-sized saucepan and cook the chopped onion, garlic and ginger over a moderate heat for about 10 minutes, stirring regularly. Meanwhile, bring the chicken stock to the boil and add the soy sauce.

When the onion is soft, add the rice and cook, stirring frequently for 3 minutes, then add a few ladles of the hot stock, stirring all the time.

Add another ladle of stock as the last one is absorbed – you should always just be able to see liquid at the top. Continue stirring and adding hot stock until the rice is cooked but still a little bit firm.

While the rice is cooking, trim the tough stems off the mushrooms and cut the caps into thick slices. Melt 15g (½oz) of the butter in a saucepan over medium heat with 2 tbsp each of chicken stock and soy sauce and the sugar. Add the sliced mushrooms and simmer gently for 2 minutes – but don't forget to stir the rice regularly as this gives the risotto its delicious creamy texture.

When the rice is cooked, stir in the remaining butter, along with the spring onions and fresh coriander. Ladle generously into warm bowls and top with a few tablespoons of the shiitake mushrooms in their sauce.

Paul Rankin

Paul initially trained with Albert Roux at Michelin three starred Le Gavroche, before returning to Belfast in 1989 to set up his first restaurant and revolutionising the dining experience in Northern Ireland. His flagship restaurant Cayenne has received praise from all corners of the globe. Paul also operates Café Paul Rankin with numerous locations throughout Northern Ireland, Rain City, a neighbourhood diner situated in Belfast's university quarter and at Junction One, Antrim. Paul and his wife, Jeanne, appeared together on their television culinary journey Gourmet Ireland accompanied by two books in the mid-1990s. *New Irish Cookery* is their latest publication, a compilation of simple Irish dishes with a modern twist. Paul has gone on to front *The Rankin Challenge* with appearances on *MasterChef, Who'll do the Pudding?, The Good Food Show* and *Ready Steady Cook.*

Paul Gayler

Szechuan Hot Fried Vegetables with Spicy Bean Sauce

You could try other combinations of vegetables here, as long as you choose contrasting colours and textures. The heat comes from Chinese black bean sauce – an easy way of spicing up stir-fries and other oriental dishes.

Serves 4

3 tbsp sesame oil
1 garlic clove, crushed
2.5cm (1inch) piece of fresh root ginger, finely chopped
2 Japanese aubergines, sliced
1 carrot, sliced
1 green and 1 red pepper, cut into 1cm (½in) dice
100g (4oz) sugarsnap peas
225g (8oz) choi sum (Chinese flowering cabbage), trimmed
12 fresh or canned water chestnuts (peeled if fresh), sliced
1 tbsp ketjap manis (Indonesian soy sauce)
1 tsp cornflour, blended with 2 tsp cold water
100ml (3½fl oz) black bean sauce
75g (3oz) cashew nuts
Salt and freshly ground black pepper

Heat the oil in a wok or a large frying pan, add the garlic and ginger and leave to infuse for 30 seconds. Add the vegetables and water chestnuts and stir-fry for about 3-4 minutes, until crisp and tender. Add the ketjap manis and cornflour paste and stir-fry until the vegetables are glazed in the soy sauce. Add the black bean sauce and 150ml (¼ pint) of water and bring to the boil, then season to taste. Transfer to a serving bowl, scatter on the cashews and serve.

Sonia Stevenson

Aubergine Sandpot

Asian aubergines come in all shapes, sizes and colours. They range from tiny, green grape-like bunches to the egg-shaped white ones which gave them one of their common names "egg plant" and from the familiar large purple kinds to the Chinese varieties about 7cm long which are ideal for this recipe. Alternative vegetables can include okra, baby leeks or shredded turnips

Serves 4

1 small aubergine or 4 Chinese ones
200g broccoli
1 carrot, cut in batons
1½ tsp sugar
1½ tsp salt
3 tbsp peanut oil
1 tbsp sesame oil
3cm fresh ginger, scraped
and sliced
2 garlic cloves crushed
240g canned waterchestnuts, rinsed and drained
1 tbsp yellow bean paste thinned with 6 tbsp water
1 tbsp dark soy sauce
1 tbsp rice vinegar
125ml vegetable stock
2 tsp cornflour, mixed with 1 tbsp water
2 spring onions, finely sliced

Trim and cut the aubergine into finger strip batons, and put aside. Remove the flower heads from the broccoli, put aside. Peel the broccoli stalk and cut into similar sized batons as the aubergine. Do the same to the carrots.

Bring a large saucepan of water to the boil, then add ½ teaspoon of the salt and ½ teaspoon of the sugar. Add the broccoli florets and blanch for 2 minutes. Remove them with a slotted spoon and refresh in a bowl of cold water. Add the broccoli stems and carrots to the boiling water and blanch for 5 minutes. Remove them with a slotted spoon and add to the bowl of cold water to refresh them, then drain the vegetables through a colander, but reserve their cooking water.

Put the peanut oil and 1 teaspoon of the sesame oil into a wok, add the ginger and garlic and stir fry for two minutes. Add the aubergines and fry for a further two minutes. Add the drained vegetables and water chestnuts and stir fry for two minutes to coat with the oil and make them glisten. Transfer to a sandpot or other casserole.

Add the remaining sesame oil to the wok, then add the diluted yellow bean paste, soy sauce, vinegar, stock, the remaining sugar and salt and 125ml of the blanching water. Bring to the boil. Mix the cornflour with 1 tablespoon of water then stir into the wok.

Pour over the vegetables and sprinkle with sliced spring onions. Cover and transfer to a heated oven at 350°F, 180°C, Gas Mark 4 and cook for 20 minutes or until the liquid bubbles through. Serve with rice.

Taken from *Casseroles* published by Ryland Peters & Small 2001

Sarah Jane Evans

Spicy Potatoes

These potatoes add spice to any number of Western foods – fish, meat, chicken. I also cook them as a delicious vegetable dish in an array of curries. Serve it with plain yoghurt and the contrast of crispy, crunchy poppadums.

Serves 4-6

1kg potatoes, scrubbed (and peeled if you prefer)
3 tbsp sunflower oil
½ tsp cumin seeds
¼ tsp fenugreek seeds
Piece of ginger about 8cm x 3cm, peeled and grated
450g tin chopped tomatoes
1 tsp ground cumin
1 tsp ground coriander
¼ - ½ tsp chilli powder (or more to taste)

Chop the potatoes into small chunks, and steam or boil until cooked. Heat the oil in a large, solid frying pan and when hot add the cumin and fenugreek seeds. Stir, then add the ginger, stir again and add the tomatoes. Allow to cook for 2-3 minutes, then stir in the ground cumin, coriander and chilli and stir well. Add the potatoes. Stir in up to 250ml water as necessary and bring to the boil. Simmer, covered, for 10-15 minutes until the potatoes are coated with a rich sauce.

Kaha Bath – Yellow Rice

Fritz Zwahlen

3 cups basmati or long grain rice
50g butter or ghee
2pc red onions sliced finely
1 lemon grass stalk cut in half and pounded slightly
1 clove garlic sliced finely
5cm fresh turmeric root, peeled and sliced finely
12 curry leaves

spices
1pc cinnamon stick
6 pods cardamom pounded
20 whole peppercorns
8 whole cloves

seasonings
10g sea salt
4 whole pandan leaves*
4 cups coconut cream
water to cover

Wash the rice thoroughly in several changes of water.

Heat the butter in a large heavy based pan and fry the onions and garlic until browned. Add the curry leaves, turmeric and lemon grass and all spices, fry for a few seconds. Add the washed rice and continue to stir until the rice is well coated with butter and spices. Add the salt, coconut cream and pandan leaves, stir well. Add water to cover the rice by 1cm, stir and cover with a lid.

Cook on a high heat until most of the water has been absorbed by the rice.

When the rice is cooked – about 20 minutes, fluff the rice well with a fork and serve hot with chopped coriander if desired.

** Lime leaves or bay leaves can be used in place of pandan leaves.*

Rachel McGuinness

Rachel McGuinness always had an appreciation of cookery and eating good food from an early age, and went on to study hospitality management in the early 1980's. Rachel worked in hotels and private residences in Europe. Then, after a spell in the airline catering industry, she spent the next decade organising lavish events in Europe for the telecoms industry.
Two years ago she gave up her corporate jet set life, and set up her own health and fitness consultancy called 'The Life Spa', where clients keep fit and lose weight through sensible eating following her program of recipes.

Scallop & Lime Risotto with a Tamarind Drizzle

Serves 4 for a main course or could serve 6 for a starter

For the tamarind drizzle

this can be prepared up to 2 hours before you make the risotto.

- 2 tbsp tamarind paste
- 4 tbsp warm water
- 1 tbsp olive oil
- 1 tsp sesame oil
- 2 garlic cloves, finely chopped
- 1 red chilli, deseeded and finely chopped
- 2.5cm piece ginger, grated
- 1 tbsp Asian fish sauce
- 2 tsp brown sugar
- 2 tbsp coriander, finely chopped

In a bowl dissolve the tamarind in the warm water by gently mashing with a fork. Pass the mixture through a sieve into another bowl – discard any solids.

Heat the olive and sesame oils together in a small pan over a moderate heat. Add the garlic, chilli and ginger and fry gently until soft. Add the tamarind mix, fish sauce and brown sugar.

Simmer for around 3-5 minutes until thickened to a light syrup.

Allow to cool for 15 minutes and then add the chopped coriander.

For the risotto

- 2 tbsp olive oil
- 1 shallot or small onion, finely chopped
- 1 clove of garlic, finely chopped
- 230g good quality Arborio rice
- 3 limes, juice and zest
- 200ml white wine
- 1 litre chicken or vegetable stock, simmering
- salt and freshly ground black pepper
- 2 tbsp coriander, finely chopped

Heat the olive oil in a heavy based pan over a moderate heat.

Gently fry the onion and garlic in the olive oil until soft, but not coloured, for about 5 minutes.

Add the rice and stir constantly for about 2 minutes. Add the white wine and keep stirring until it has been absorbed by the rice. Stir in the lime juice. Add a ladleful of the stock and bring to a gentle boil, reduce the heat to a simmer.

Cook, slowly, stirring frequently until the liquid has been absorbed. Repeat this gradual addition of stock until the rice is creamy and tender, but with a little bite (al dente) and season to taste - this should take between 15 - 18 minutes.

Stir in the chopped coriander and lime zest just before serving to retain all the flavours

Scallops

24 fresh scallops

Use the freshest scallops possible, clean the scallops under fresh running water, and dry on some kitchen towel (You will be cooking them in a hot pan with oil, so they must be as dry as possible)

1 tsp olive oil

Sea salt and freshly ground black pepper

Heat the oil in a large non-stick frying pan over a high heat.

Carefully place each scallop in the pan. If the pan is hot enough, the scallop will "sear" immediately, and get a nice brown caramelisation on it.

Cook the scallops for about one minute, season then turn them over.

Cook for a further 2 minutes on the other side, and again season.

NOTE: Do not over cook the scallops or they will become tough, they need to be barely cooked through.

To serve

Arrange 3 spoonfuls of risotto on plate.

Place 2 scallops on each mound of risotto

Carefully drizzle the tamarind sauce around the plate.

Tip: Garnish with stir fried bok choi for a bit of extra colour.

Peter Gordon

Kumara, Feta and Smoked Paprika Tortilla

Tortilla is the Spanish name for what is often called a Spanish omelette or as the Italians say – a frittata. Kumara is the native sweet potato of New Zealand – it is available in the UK sporadically, but if you can't find it then you can replace it with regular sweet potato. Simply serve this with a salad and crusty bread.

Serves 6

300g kumara, peeled and cut into 1cm cubes
200g potatoes, peeled and cut into 1cm cubes
2 tsp spicy smoked paprika
200ml extra virgin olive oil
1 large red onion, peeled and finely sliced
50ml sherry vinegar or balsamic vinegar
10 large eggs
125g feta, roughly crumbled
3 spring onions, finely sliced
1½ tsp sea salt
freshly ground pepper

Preheat oven to 200°C. Mix kumara and potatoes with paprika and half the oil. Lay on a roasting tray and bake until potatoes are just cooked. Meanwhile, fry onion in 2 tablespoons of the oil until caramelised. Add vinegar and cook until it evaporates. Crack the eggs into a bowl and lightly whisk, then add the onion and kumara mixtures, along with the oil they were cooked in. Add the feta, spring onions, salt and pepper and mix well.

Heat a 24 cm ovenproof frying pan, add remaining oil and when it begins to smoke (just a few seconds) add the egg mixture all at once. Leave to bubble for 10 seconds, then shake (or toss if you're feeling confident), bringing the cooked outer reaches into the centre and the runny centre to the outside. Do this a few times then turn heat down and cook for one minute.

Transfer to the top shelf of the oven and cook 8–10 minutes. It's ready when the eggs are just set; overcooked eggs go tough. Cool for five minutes then give the pan a gentle shake to loosen the tortilla, using a blunt knife to help if needed. Invert onto a plate. Let it cool before serving as it tastes best after an hour or so. Otherwise, let it cool then covering with cling-film and storing in the fridge for no more than 2 days.

Taken from *A World in my Kitchen* published by Hodder Moa Beckett (NZ) 2003

Notes

Notes

BAKING

Mary Berry

Mary Berry is best known for her Aga cooking workshops which over 13,000 Aga owners have attended. *The Mail on Sunday YOU Magazine* said: "Mary Berry is to Aga what Pavarotti is to opera!" Well known to both television and radio audiences, Mary is also the author of over 60 cookery books with total sales of over 5 million copies. With her daughter Annabel she produces the *Mary Berry & Daughter* range of salad dressings and sauces which are sold everywhere from farm shops to Fortnums. It is a family business so her husband is heavily involved too.

Fresh Raspberry Scones

Fresh blueberries can replace the raspberries if wished but we prefer the raspberries! The scone dough is very deep to cut out once layered with the raspberries, so flour the cutter well between each cutting to prevent the dough sticking. The large scone made from the trimmings is perfect sliced for the family.

450g (1lb) self-raising flour
4 tsp baking powder
100g (4oz) butter
50g (2oz) caster sugar
2 eggs
milk
about 100g (4oz) fresh raspberries

Lightly grease 2 baking trays. Preheat the oven to 220°C/425°F/Gas Mark 7.

Measure the flour and baking powder into a large bowl. Add the butter and rub in with the fingertips until the mixture resembles fine breadcrumbs. Stir in the sugar.

Break the eggs into a measuring jug, then make up to 300ml (10fl oz) with milk. Stir the egg and milk into the flour – you may not need it all – and mix to a soft but not sticky dough.

Turn out onto a lightly floured work surface, knead lightly and then roll out to a rectangle about 2cm (¾ inch) thick. Cut the rectangle of dough into two equal pieces.

Scatter the fresh raspberries evenly over one piece of dough. Top with the second rectangle of dough. Cut into as many rounds as possible with a fluted 5cm (2 inch) cutter (see tip) and place them on the prepared baking trays. Gently push the trimmings together to form one large scone, score the top with a sharp knife. Brush the tops of the scones with a little extra milk, or any egg and milk left in the jug.

Bake in the preheated oven for about 15 minutes or until the scones are well risen and a pale golden brown. (The large scone will need about a further 5 minutes). Lift onto a wire rack to cool. Eat as fresh as possible.

Makes about 12 small scones

To prepare ahead

Best eaten on the day of making. If you must, store in the fridge for a day once made, reheat to serve.

To freeze / thaw

These freeze extremely well. Freeze the cooled scones in plastic bags for up to 6 months. Thaw in the plastic bags for 2-3 hours at room temperature, reheat to serve.

To reheat / serve

Refresh in a preheated oven at 200°C/400°F/Gas Mark 6 for about 3 minutes.

To cook in the Aga

Cook on the grid shelf on the lowest set of runners of the roasting oven for about 10-15 minutes.

Taken from *Cook Now Eat Later* published by Headline 2003

Lady Holmes

Penny Holmes is the wife of the British Ambassador in Paris. Along with Monsieur James Viaene, who has been the Residence Chef for over 35 years, she spends a lot of her time working on ways to promote British food in France. On the Ambassador's lunch and dinner menus there are familiar dishes such as Lancashire Hotpot, Bubble and Squeak and Apple Crumble, and a Victoria Sponge or homemade biscuits served with afternoon tea for guests. She and a friend, Susan Mallet, have recently produced a book of British recipes in French called *Simply British* (Marabout). The proceeds from the book go to research into breast cancer both in France and Britain.

Lemon Victoria Sponge

6oz softened butter (170g)
6oz caster sugar (170g)
6oz self raising flour (170g)
1 tsp baking powder
3 large eggs
Grated rind of 1 lemon plus 1 dessertspoon of juice

Set the oven to 170°C (325°F or Gas Mark 3)

Lightly grease two 8 inch (20cm) sponge tins (1in/2.5cm deep) and line the base with a circle of baking parchment.

Sift flour and baking powder into a large bowl. Add all the other ingredients and whisk with an electric whisk until well mixed. The mixture should fall off a wooden spoon easily when tapped on the edge of the bowl. If not, add 1 teaspoon of warm water and whisk again.

Divide the mixture between the two tins, making the mixture level. Bake in centre of the oven for about 30 minutes. The cake should feel springy to the touch. Turn out on to a cooling rack and peel off the papers.

When cool, sandwich the two cakes together with lemon curd (adding a little fresh cream for a special event) and sprinkle the top with icing sugar through a fine sieve.

Eat as fresh as possible!

Spiced Apple Cake

4oz butter or margarine
8oz raisins or sultanas
1 stewed apple
1 cup of strong tea (ceylon)
8oz self raising flour
4oz castor sugar or granulated
½ tsp of mixed spice
½ tsp of bicarb of soda
1 egg

Butter a round tin (7") and line bottom and side with greaseproof paper.

Melt butter in saucepan, add raisins and tea and bring to the boil. Allow to simmer for 2 minutes, then cool. Mix other ingredients, pour into tin, and put in oven for 1¼ hours at Gas Mark 4/350°F/180°C.

'Mixed spice' contains ground mace, coriander, caraway, cassia, cloves, ginger, cinnamon and pimento

Sharon Evans

Sharon Evans is currently based in Sri Lanka and co-ordinated the medical aid and counselling support provided by the British High Commission in Colombo for British nationals following the Tsunami. As President of the British Welfare Group, she is now helping to raise money to assist Sri Lankan victims of the disaster. Born in Adelaide, South Australia Sharon qualified as a nurse and midwife before starting to travel the world. To date she has lived in eight countries picking up further qualifications, including counselling, on the way. Married with three grown-up children her interests are travel, sport, art, music, dance and reading philosophy.

Jane Asher

Jane Asher is an actress, writer and businesswoman. She runs her own business, "Jane Asher Party Cakes & Sugarcraft", and has developed the *Jane Asher* range of cake mixes, which is a best selling brand. Her most recent theatre appearance was in *Festen* at the Lyric Theatre in London. She also recently appeared in an episode of *Miss Marple* on ITV. Jane has also written three best-selling novels. Jane's work in the charity field is well respected. She is President of the National Autistic Society and Arthritis Care, Vice-President of the Child Accident Prevention Trust and the National Deaf Children's Society.

Rich Chocolate Cake

125g (4oz) plain chocolate
125g (4oz) softened butter
125g (4oz) caster sugar
5 egg yolks
4 egg whites
1 tsp vanilla essence
125g (4oz) self raising flour
Apricot jam

For the glaze
250g (8oz) dark chocolate, finely chopped or grated
4fl oz (100ml) double cream

You will need an 8 inch (20cm) deep cake tin, greased and floured

Cream the butter and one third of the sugar, then add the egg yolks, beating continuously. Melt the chocolate in a bowl over a saucepan of simmering water or in a microwave, then let it cool slightly. Fold the vanilla essence and warm chocolate into the egg/sugar mix. Whisk the egg whites until stiff, then beat in the remaining sugar. Alternately fold the egg white and sifted flour into the chocolate mix, then pour into the cake tin and bake at 180°C/350°F/Gas Mark 4 for 40-50 minutes, checking after 40 minutes by inserting a skewer into the middle – if it comes out clean the cake is cooked. When cool split the sponge in half and spread with a layer of apricot jam.

To prepare the glaze

In a saucepan bring the cream to the boil and pour it over the grated chocolate. Stir until it is all melted. Allow to cool slightly.

Place the cake onto a cooling rack over a large plate or oven tray and pour over the glaze, scooping up excess from the plate with a spatula, making sure the glaze completely covers the cake and goes all the way down the sides.

Welsh Tea Bread

A taste of childhood always made for me by a favourite aunt and one I have served in all the countries we have been posted to.

110g raisins
110g sultanas
110g currants
110g Demerara sugar
140ml hot English Breakfast tea
50g chopped walnuts
1 egg, beaten
225g self-raising flour

1 x 450g loaf tin, greased & floured

Dissolve the sugar in the hot tea and pour over the dried fruit. Cover and leave for 12 hours.

Pre-heat oven to Gas Mark 3, 170°C and grease and flour loaf tin.

Add beaten egg to dried fruit mixture.

Sift in the flour and add nuts.

Mix well and pour into loaf tin.

Bake for 1-1¼ hours until skewer comes out cleanly or springy to touch.

Serve thinly sliced and spread lightly with butter.

Enid Humfrey

As a Welsh-born diplomat's wife, Enid Humfrey has spent the last 33 years entertaining a stream of guests of every nationality, age group and dietary whim. In her last posting, when her husband Charles was British Ambassador in Seoul, they entertained over 20,000 official guests in functions large and small in 3 years. In the interstices in Tokyo, New York, Ankara, Seoul and now Jakarta, she has brought up three children, taught English literature at universities, tutored a Princess, given talks on British cooking for television and written a cookery book for a British Festival. She is now raising and distributing funds for tsunami relief in Aceh.

Darina Allen

Roscommon Rhubarb Tart

This delectable tart is an adaptation of a traditional recipe which was originally cooked in a bastable over the open fire – everyone adores it. One could also add a couple of teaspoons of freshly grated ginger to the rhubarb, but try it unadorned at first, it's seriously good.

Serves 8-10 • In season: late spring

900g (2lb) red rhubarb
255-285g (9-10oz) granulated sugar
55g (2oz) butter
1 egg
175ml (6fl oz) full cream milk, approx

Topping
310g (11oz) flour
20g (¾oz) castor sugar
1 heaped tsp baking powder
pinch of salt
egg wash
granulated sugar

Grease a 23x5cm (9x2inch) round tin. We use a heavy stainless steel sauté pan which works very well, if you don't have a suitable pan, part cook the rhubarb slightly first. Preheat the oven to 230°C/450°F.

Trim the rhubarb, wipe with a damp cloth and cut into pieces about 2.5cm (1inch) in length. Put into the base of a tin or sauté pan, sprinkle with the sugar. We put the stainless steel sauté pan on a low heat at this point while we make the dough.

Sieve all the dry ingredients into a bowl. Cut the butter into cubes and rub into the flour until the mixture resembles coarse breadcrumbs. Whisk the egg with the milk. Make a well in the centre of the dry ingredients, pour in the liquid all at once and mix to a soft dough. Turn out onto a floured board and roll into a 23cm (9inch) round about 2.5cm (1inch) thick. Place this round on top of the rhubarb and tuck in the edges neatly. Brush with a little egg wash and sprinkle with granulated sugar.

Bake in the fully preheated oven for 15 minutes then reduce the temperature to 180°C/350°F for a further 30 minutes approx. or until the top is crusty and golden and the rhubarb soft and juicy.

Remove from the oven and allow to sit for a few minutes. Put a warm plate over the top of the sauté pan, turn upside down onto the plate but be careful of the hot juices.

Serve warm with soft brown sugar and cream.

Apple and Cinnamon Tarte Tatin

Use 675g (1½lb) dessert apples, peeled and dried. Mix 1 teaspoon freshly ground cinnamon with 140g (5oz) castor sugar and sprinkle over the apples and continue as above.

Sugar and Spice Tarte Tatin

Substitute 1 teaspoon of mixed spice for cinnamon in the above recipe.

Taken from Darina Allen's *Irish Traditional Cooking* published by Kyle Cathie
www.cookingisfun.ie

Jane Asher

Everyday Gingerbread

METRIC	IMPERIAL
450g plain flour	1lb plain flour
5ml salt	1 level tsp salt
15ml ground ginger	1 level tbsp ground ginger
15ml baking powder	1 level tbsp baking powder
5ml bicarbonate of soda	1 level tsp bicarbonate of soda
225g demerara sugar	8oz demerara sugar
175g butter	6oz butter
175g black treacle	6oz black treacle
175g golden syrup	6oz golden syrup
250ml milk	½ pt milk
1 beaten medium egg	1 beaten medium egg

Grease and line a 9 inch square cake tin. Sift the flour, salt, ginger, baking powder and bicarbonate of soda. Warm the sugar, fat, treacle and syrup until melted, but don't allow to boil. Mix in the milk and the egg. Add the liquid and mix well. Pour the mix into the tin and bake at 170°C (325°F) Gas Mark 3 for about an hour and a half. Turn out to cool on a wire rack.

(To make a smaller cake, use half the quantities and bake for an hour or so)

Lemon And Lime Traybake

Mary Berry

For a special occasion, or if the limes are a reasonable price, you could use the juice and rind of 6 limes for a really fresh taste, omitting the lemon.

275g (10oz) self-raising flour
225g (8oz) caster sugar
4 eggs
225g (8oz) baking margarine, at room temperature
2 tsp baking powder
finely grated rind of 2 lemons
finely grated rind of 2 limes
2 tbsp milk

For the topping

175g (6oz) granulated sugar
juice of 2 limes and 1 lemon

Line a 30 x 23 cm (12 x 9 inch) traybake tin with foil and grease well. Pre-heat the oven to 180°C / 350°F / Gas Mark 4.

Measure all of the cake ingredients into a large bowl and mix well using an electric beater. Spoon into the prepared tin and gently level the top. Bake in the pre-heated oven for 30-35 minutes or until well risen and pale golden brown.

Mix together the sugar and lime and lemon juices for the topping and pour over the warm cake. Allow to cool. Cuts into 21 pieces.

To prepare ahead
Weigh out the ingredients and line the tin. Bake and complete the cake and store in an airtight container for 2-3 days.

To freeze / thaw
Leave whole. Pack and freeze for up to 2 months. Thaw at room temperature for 2-3 hours. Cut into squares to serve.

To cook in the Aga
2 oven Aga: Bake on the lowest set of runners in the roasting oven and slide the cold sheet on the second set of runners. Bake for about 30-35 minutes until pale golden brown and shrinking away from the sides of the tin.

4 oven Aga: Bake on the grid shelf on the floor of the baking oven for 30-35 minutes. After 20 minutes if the cake is getting too brown, slide the cold shelf on the second set of runners.

Taken from *Cook Now Eat Later* published by Headline 2003

Lady Holmes

Chef's Ginger Biscuits

110g flour
1 tsp bicarbonate of soda
1 tsp ginger powder (a little rounded according to taste)
2 tbsp Golden Syrup
40g caster sugar
50g butter

Preheat oven to 350°F (180°C) Gas Mark 4 and lightly grease a baking sheet.

Sieve the flour with the bicarbonate of soda and ginger powder. Add castor sugar, butter and the golden syrup. (Chef adds a pinch of vanilla powder to the mixture to bring out the flavours). Mix well to form a paste.

Make little balls in your hand from a teaspoon of the mixture.

Put the balls on the baking sheet at 10cm intervals. With the palm of your hand, press them down into rounds 5mm thick.

Put in the oven at 180°C for 7 or 8 minutes until the biscuits are a golden colour.

Take out and cool on a wire tray. Store in a good airtight tin as they soften easily.

Delicious with pineapple ice cream or souffle OR just on their own!

Apple Amber

Tessa Bramley

This is a fabulous yet simple alternative to lemon meringue pie. Choose a type of dessert apple which will break down during cooking to make a rough puree. I prefer to have some texture in the filling rather than a smooth puree. You could, of course, use cooking apples, but then you would also need to increase the amount of sugar you used to make the puree. If you don't like the flavour of cardamom you could use 3 or 4 cloves instead. These are best removed after making the filling. Since the flavour of clove is so strong you really only want a hint of it in the apple.

225g rich buttery short crust pastry

Line a 20cm loose-bottomed flan tin with the pastry and then bake blind at 200°C, Gas Mark 6, for 20 minutes, removing baking beans for the last 5 minutes to dry out the pastry.

8 large dessert apples – peeled, cored and chopped
3 strips lemon zest
3 tbsp water
juice of ½ lemon
the seeds from 12 crushed green cardamom pods
2 to 3 tbsp caster sugar to taste (leave slightly tart because of the sweetness of the meringue)
3 large eggs – separated carefully

Cook together the apples, flavourings, sugar and water until softened to a coarse pulp. Remove strips of zest and discard. Beat the egg yolks and add to the puree. Pour into cooked and cooled pastry case.

Meringue topping
Re-set oven temp to 130°C, Gas Mark ¼ and allow it to cool down to this before baking the meringue topped tart.
3 egg whites plus a pinch of salt
4 tbsp caster sugar
1 dessertspoon of corn flour
2 tsp of lemon juice
½ tbsp of extra caster sugar to sprinkle on top

Whisk egg whites with the salt until stiff. Whisk in 1 tbsp of sugar until glossy and stiffly peaked. Whisk in the rest of the sugar in two lots and keep whisking to bring back to stiff peaks each time. Sprinkle over the corn flour and lemon juice and gently fold in – I like to use the whisk for this. Using a large spoon, pile the meringue on top of the apple filling, leaving the meringue in rough peaks. Sprinkle with the remaining sugar.

Bake in a cool oven for about an hour until the meringue is crisp on the outside with the peaks just tinged golden. The centre of the meringue will be fluffy and marshmallow like.

Notes

Notes

Matt Skinner

Matt Skinner hails from Melbourne, Australia where in 2002 he was invited by Jamie Oliver to head-up wine at Fifteen and teach the subject to its students. Over the years, Matt has put pen to paper for publications such as *Wine X*, *Wine*, *GQ*, *BBC Good Food* and *Delicious*. He is a regular guest on UK Food TV's 'Great Food Live', and is wine editor of jamieoliver.com – the world's most visited non-commercial food website. Matt has recently completed his first book *Thirsty Work*, due for publication by Mitchell-Beazley in September 2005. He lives, works and plays in London.

Hot food, cool wine

A major slice of wine's magic is in knowing that there's always something new happening somewhere - a new region, a new producer, a new variety, a new style - a completely new way of doing something that's probably been done much the same way for donkey's years. In the great big world of wine there's rarely - if ever - a dull moment and for me that means an anticipation of tasting something that I've never tried before, meeting the people who hammered it together, travelling to where the wine was made, and discovering (mainly through loads of trial and error!) which food styles will work best with the new kid on the block.

Nowadays, far too much noise is made about the 'the importance of food and wine matching'. Have fun playing around with combinations, but never let them get in the way of sharing and enjoying a good meal. The most important thing to know is 'knowing what you like'. If a particular combination works for you, bingo, that's all that should matter. Like bread and butter, Lennon and McCartney, Schumacher and his shiny red Ferrari - some things were meant to be together. Food and wine matching is the same. Some work, some don't – but half the fun is in the trying!

So how do we get started then?

Ok. To better illustrate the relationship between food and wine I need you to picture a pair of tartan pants. A blur of blue, red, black and white. Not the smoothest look I know, but work with me here! Team it with a red shirt, and you'll notice that all the red checks on the pants stand out, while the other colours fall into a messy blur. Some colours in the pants are amplified, while others are dulled. Put on a white shirt and the same things happen but with white checks. Match them with a spotted shirt of brown and orange and not only are the colours all wrong but the patterns make you look like a dog's breakfast – worse still, your reflection is enough to give even a mirror a headache! Mix them with a shiny satin shirt and now the textures are all over the shop too...

Food and wine are the same — the flavour of each is made up of many different components, and which shirt – sorry - partner you choose, will determine what part of the food or wine is amplified or contrasted, muted or matched. See? Enhance the subtleties of your wine and bring out the best in your food. Jancis Robinson hit the nail on the head when she said, 'Surely well chosen wine makes ordinary food taste better'!

Getting down to business.

For food and wine pairing to work you'll need to know a bit about what you're eating, how it feels in your mouth once it's cooked or prepared, and what the key flavours are. Having a similar understanding about what you're drinking — reds compared to whites, a lighter pinot compared to a big gutsy Shiraz - is also going to be invaluable.

The old approach to food and wine matching – which probably says more about how seriously we used to take food and wine culture - was simply red meat=red wine, and everything else goes with white. But remember this. It's not so much about the wine's colour as it is about the balance of flavours and textures of both the food and wine when combined. This is the foundation for any good food and wine match. Get to grips with that and you're going to romp it in!

So, breaking it all down then...

Weight: First and foremost you want to try to match the weight of both the food and wine so that one doesn't overpower the other. This way the subtleties and best parts of each are highlighted rather than pushed to one side and ruined. Now when we talk weight, we're not talking 'grams and kilograms', but rather the feel of either the food or the wine when it's in your in your mouth. Think how a cup of peppermint tea might feel compared to a pint of Guinness. Clearly the beer has a heavier and 'weightier' feel to it (not to mention a more enjoyable end result)!

A steamed piece of chicken is much lighter than the same piece of meat stuck in a casserole dish, stewed with a bottle of red wine and a whole block of butter! While the first piece of chicken could be accompanied by a glass of white, say chardonnay, the second would need something with a little more guts to get through the heartier flavours.

Acidity: Acidity in food usually comes from added sauces such as a good old squeeze of lemon on your fish, or a splash of vinegar in a salad dressing. In wine, acid most commonly comes from grapes.

Food or wine with high levels of acidity, when not matched with something of equal levels of acid, will overpower the other. The acid in a dish needs to be equalled by the acid in the wine otherwise one will seem flat and dull. It's like playing tennis with two players of equal skill — it's a much better game if Hewitt's up against Safin than if he's playing against your cousin who just scored his first tennis racket for Christmas — one would simply annihilate the other!

To ensure this rule is not so simple, there are a couple of exceptions. Gentle levels of acidity in white wine can also make a simple dish a bit livelier as might the 'good old squeeze of lemon on our fish'. Also, a gentle creamy dish might go well with a slightly acidic wine as a contrast to cut through the cream.

Salt: Not just bad for the ticker, too much salt in a dish will also have a negative effect on the wine. You see, much of a wine's flavour comes from the fruit sweetness. When you add loads of salt to this, all that lovely fruit will be overshadowed, leaving you with a pretty average impression of the flavours in the wine.

Sweetness: Again this is about matching things, in this case flavours, of equal proportions. Very sweet food will make a wine bland because all that sugar will override the qualities of the wine. This will make the wine seem dull, like taking away David Beckham's tattoos — you just end up with a good football player.

Texture: Different to weight, texture is 'what you feel' in your mouth. Picture a bowl full of peaches and cream. Both share very different textures, yet are completely complementary to one another. The same principles apply to food and wine, and your chosen food can completely contrast the texture of your wine without creating a clash.

Balance: Get all the above bits right, and this one – perhaps the most important part of the subject – should just fall into place all by itself. Balance is the combination of all the above components working together in harmony. Think about a set of seesaw where on one side you have food, and the other wine – the idea being to get the seesaw level.

Where most European cooking proves pretty straightforward for wine matching, Southeast Asian and Chinese cookery definitely doesn't. Designed to contrast a mixture of flavours and textures, Asian cooking concentrates on four key cornerstones; sweet, sour, salty, and hot – a minefield for wine lovers!

Asian food and wine matching defies convention and I love that. The fact that you can throw the rulebook out the window is a breath of fresh air. I try to look at the overall construction of the dish, and, from experience, wines that can handle at least two or three of the 'key cornerstones' will work best.

To make the process a little less painful, I've included some of my favourite wine styles to enjoy with a range of Asian foods below.

Fizz: Unfortunately, Champagne and sparkling wine's compatibility with many Asian ingredients is way too brief and all too limited for my liking! Texture is the key here, with high acid fizz providing a brilliant vehicle for cleaning your palate of anything remotely fatty and/or salty. Salt and pepper squid, deep fried scallops, tempura - anything lightly fried or battered are obvious candidates for fizz. But where Champagne and sparkling wine struggle, another member of the fizz family, sparkling Shiraz, reigns supreme. So what's it like then? Picture a big, rich, chunky red wine – only picture it fizzy and served cold! Sound good? And with most sparkling reds relying on Shiraz as the star variety of choice, the additional hint of sweetness and a good dose of tannin mean that in all but a few cases, these are wines that should work brilliantly with anything sweet, sour, hot or sticky.

Aromatic whites : It's amongst this family – the aromatic whites - that you'll kick the most goals. Varieties such as Sauvignon Blanc, Pinot Grigio/Gris, Muscadet, and Gewürztraminer are all worthy soldiers, but at the end of the day none quite stack up like Riesling. And Riesling – particularly the Germanic style - has it all. Delicate fruit flavours, low alcohol, lively acid, and a touch of residual sugar will all rise to the occasion when paired with assorted steamed dumplings, all the usual deep fried suspects, glutenous rice, slippery hand stretched noodles, and a cast of sauces.

Bigger whites: Fans of bigger whites should look away now. Sorry to have to report it, but with most Asian food styles, these kind of wines just don't cut it. Extra body in wine usually comes as a result of extra alcohol, which is where our problems begin. Dry wines with both high acidity and alcohol will prove nasty partners with spice – especially chilli. But there's always an exception to any rule, and Viognier has proven its worth as a serious partner to many Southeast Asian and Chinese food styles. High in alcohol/low in acidity, much of Viognier's attraction lies in its highly exotic aromatics and oily mouth feel.

Pink wines: I'm never happier than on Sunday mornings sitting up at Yum Cha - my all-time favourite meal – chopsticks in one hand, glass of rose in the other! It's a fact that many pink wines come with the combination of residual sweetness and the faintest lick of tannin that make them so versatile with light and delicate dumplings all the way through to steamed chicken's feet with black bean and ginger!

Lightweight reds: Like Homer and his beloved Doughnuts, Pinot and Duck combine to make a truly undeniable combination. Simple fruit flavours, gentle acid and silky tannins combine to cut through and complement sweet and gamey meat and the fatty, mouth-watering skin of the duck.

Great big reds: Few big reds fit the bill with many Southeast Asian and Chinese ingredients due to excessive amounts of flavour, tannin, and alcohol. Think big flavours to match these wines. Sauces such as Hoi Sin, Char Sui, and smoked or barbequed meats are great with combinations of Grenache, Syrah and Mourvedre which sport dark fruit and spice, moderate acidity and gentle tannin. Beware of wines that are carrying large amounts of alcohol and tannin which will simply prove too much for many dishes.

DESSERTS

Ross Burden

Steamed Ginger Pudding

Classic comfort food from Ross Burden, with his meltingly moist, delicately flavoured steamed ginger pudding topped with stem ginger.

Serves 6 • preparation 20 minutes • cooking 2 hours

Butter, for greasing
100g shredded suet
75g caster sugar
200g plain flour
1 tsp ground ginger
1 tsp bicarbonate of soda
1 tbsp black treacle, warmed
1 egg, beaten
50-100ml milk

To serve
knob of preserved stem ginger, chopped
thick cream or custard

Grease a 1-litre pudding bowl with butter and prepare a saucepan large enough to take the bowl comfortably.

Put the suet and sugar in a large mixing bowl and sift the flour, ginger and bicarbonate of soda into them.

In a small mixing bowl, beat the treacle with the egg and 50ml milk. Stir this into the dry ingredients in the other bowl and add just as much extra milk as necessary to make a soft dropping consistency.

Spoon the mixture into the greased bowl, cover with greased greaseproof paper and a piece of foil, pleated to allow for expansion, secure with string or a lid if your pudding bowl has one. Stand the bowl on a saucer in the pan and pour in boiling water to come halfway up the basin.

Bring the water back to a simmer, cover tightly and steam for 2 hours, topping up the water level with more boiling water as necessary.

Remove the bowl from the pan and leave for 10 minutes to rest. Turn the pudding out on a plate, garnish with the chopped stem ginger and serve with thick cream or custard.

Taken from *Good Food Live*

Tessa Bramley

Coffee Hazelnut Pudding with a Coffee Bean Sauce

Very light little puddings with quite a sophisticated flavour. A fresh orange compote would go very well with them.

Serves 4

60g / 2oz shelled hazelnuts
60g / 2oz self raising flour
½ level tsp baking powder
pinch salt
the zest of 1 small orange - finely grated
2 tsp liquid instant coffee
120g / 4oz unsalted butter - softened
120g / 4oz brown sugar
2 eggs - beaten

You will need 4 individual pudding basins – well buttered with circles of grease proof paper in the bottom

Pre-heat oven to 160°C, 325°F, Gas Mark 3.

Grind hazelnuts in a grinder or processor. Mix with the flour, baking powder and salt

Cream together butter, sugar, zest and coffee until light and fluffy - use a food mixer to make this easier

Gradually add eggs , whisking into the mixture

Remove bowl from machine and carefully fold in flour mixture until evenly mixed. It should have a soft dropping consistency

Divide between the prepared tins and bake for about 25 minutes until well risen and firm to the touch

Run a little knife round puddings and turn out carefully onto serving plates

Pour the coffee bean sauce over and around. If you like, you can garnish the puddings with candied orange zest. Serve with orange compote.

Make the sauce whilst the puddings are baking

The sauce

Make a caramel with:-

225g caster sugar

5 tbsp water - just enough to wet the sugar

125ml strong black coffee made with freshly ground beans - I like a mix of Costa Rica and Java

1 to 2 tbsp malt whisky

5 tbsp double cream

a few coffee beans to garnish

Make caramel by dissolving the sugar in the water over a low heat. As the liquid clears, raise the heat and bring to the boil. Leave the syrup without stirring to cook to a golden caramel

Carefully pour over the coffee. Protect your hand with a cloth as the caramel will splutter and appear lumpy

Put it back on the heat and add the cream. Continue stirring until the mixture is smooth. Leave it to cook down to a coating consistency

Remove from heat and add the coffee beans and the whisky to taste.

Take the zest off 2 oranges using a zester. Put into a small pan and cover with water. Bring it to the boil to soften the zest. Drain well. Peel the remaining skin and pith from the oranges with a knife and then segment the fruit from the skin. Make a heavy syrup with 4 tablespoons each of sugar and water well reduced. Add the zest and orange segments and chill well. Serve with the puddings.

Nihal Senanayake

Nihal Senanayake is the Executive Chef of Lighthouse Hotel & Spa in Galle, Sri Lanka. He is a true local – his birth place and home being just 10 minutes away from the hotel although he has worked overseas and throughout Sri Lanka for the past 22 years. Nihal has also represented Sri Lanka Food Promotions in Hungary and Switzerland. He shares with us his special recipe for 'Watalappan' – a Sri Lankan version of 'Cream Caramel' being the easiest description.

Watalappan

Serves 15

500ml thick coconut milk
750g jaggery (palm sugar that is sold in 'cakes' in Asian shops. Muscovado sugar could be used as a substitute)
12 eggs
75ml water
50g cashew nuts
3g cardamom powder
5g nutmeg powder
3g cinnamon powder

Dissolve jaggery and water together with cardamom, nutmeg and cinnamon over a low heat. Keep 10 minutes to cool.

Slightly beat eggs and mix coconut milk together.

Mix these two mixtures together and strain through fine strainer.

Pour the mixture into a baking dish (8"x6"x2½") and add roasted cashews. Then place the dish in a baking tray with water to come three-quarters of the way up the sides of the dish.

Bake in an oven at 120°C for 1 hour. For Combi oven 45 minutes steam and heat together.

Cool and cut into portions. Chill before serving.

Donna Hay

Coconut Rice with Caramelised Banana

Serves 4

1 cup long or short-grain rice
2 cups (16fl oz) water
1 cinnamon stick
¾ cup (6fl oz) coconut cream
⅓ cup sugar

Caramelised banana
4 firm bananas, peeled and halved lengthwise
½ cup sugar
1½ tsp ground cinnamon

Place the rice in a colander and wash well. Place the rice, water and cinnamon stick in a saucepan over medium to high heat and bring to the boil. Cover tightly and reduce the heat to low and cook for 10 minutes or until the water has been absorbed. Add the coconut cream and sugar, cover the saucepan and place over very low heat for 5 minutes.

While the rice is cooking, sprinkle the bananas with the sugar and cinnamon. Preheat a non-stick frying pan over high heat. Cook the bananas for 2 minutes on each side or until the sugar has caramelised.

To serve, place the coconut rice on serving plates and top with the banana slices.

Taken from *The Instant Cook* published by Harper Collins 2004

Photo: Con Poulos

Josceline Dimbleby

A Pudding for Parvati

Serves 8 • preparation 30 minutes plus several hours chilling

Would this be fit for the Hindu goddess Parvati? I hope so. It has characteristics drawn from the many different types of Indian sweetmeats, being milky, scented and intriguingly textured, but not so intensely sweet. I am afraid that I have a very sweet tooth and I always return fatter, rather than thinner, after a visit to India. I do think that a little sharpness combines with sweetness to make an even better taste, though, which is why I often add lemon juice to Eastern-style puddings.

2 tbsp caster sugar
75g (3oz) flaked almonds
1 tsp ground cardamom
125g (4oz) semolina
6 tbsp powdered milk
900ml (1½ pints) milk
175g (6oz) demerara sugar
175g (4oz) carrots, grated
juice of 1 lemon, strained
1 tbsp rose-water

Sprinkle the caster sugar evenly over the bottom of a 1.2 litre (2 pint) capacity shallow mould or flan dish. Then sprinkle 50g (2oz) of the flaked almonds over the sugar. Heat a heavy-based saucepan over a medium heat, add the ground cardamom and stir for a moment or two to roast it. Remove the pan from the heat and after a minute or two add the semolina and powdered milk. Pour in 150ml (¼ pint) milk and stir to mix smoothly. Then add the demerara sugar and gradually stir in the remaining 750ml (1¼ pints) of milk. Now add the grated carrots. Put the pan back over a medium heat and bring to the boil, stirring all the time. Lower the heat and bubble, stirring constantly, for 10-12 minutes, until very thick. Then remove from the heat and gradually stir in the lemon juice and rose-water. Mix in the remaining 25g (1oz) flaked almonds and pour the mixture into the prepared mould or flan dish. Leave to cool and then chill thoroughly in the fridge for several hours.

To turn out, loosen the edges with your fingers and then turn on to a serving plate, giving a good shake. Now put the cake under a medium grill until it is darkly speckled on top. Chill again in the fridge before serving it cut into pieces.

Taken from Josceline Dimbleby Sainsbury Cookbooks *A Traveller's Tastes*

Photo: Carl Clemens Gros

Winter Charlotte with Rhubarb and Raspberries

A way to use good but ageing bread, that also makes use of rhubarb, a vegetable that we see as a fruit, that originated in China and has been eaten in Britain since the 16th century. Rhubarb may be seen as inexorably British; the likely candidate to find under a crumble, but once it was only loved for its cleansing effect on the gut. The best rhubarb of all is grown in Yorkshire in the winter months; forced in dark sheds where it grows fast in search of light. Its wan, pink stalks are sweet and tender. We have plenty for which to thank this particular oriental food plant. It has helped out in times of trouble, providing an essential source of fresh 'fruit' during World War II when trains of twenty carriages left Wakefield for London daily, feeding grateful, blitz weary citizens. In a charlotte, buttered day-old bread is placed on top of stewed fruit and the pudding is baked. Apples and berries make good charlottes, and it is even possible to make a savoury charlotte with chicory, apple and spices that have been slowly cooked until sweet.

Serves 6

about 8 slices of day-old white bread, crusts removed (reserve them for breadcrumbs)
softened unsalted butter
ground cinnamon
700g/1½lb forced rhubarb, cut into 2cm/¾ inch lengths
400g/14oz frozen raspberries – British are available all year round
golden caster sugar

Preheat the oven to 200°C/400°F/Gas Mark 6. Butter the bread slices and sprinkle with a little cinnamon. Cut each slice into quarters, then into 8 small triangles.

Put the rhubarb and raspberries into a pan, cover and cook over a low heat until the rhubarb is just soft. Add enough sugar to sweeten to your taste, then pour into a shallow ovenproof dish. Arrange the triangles of bread on top, buttered-side up, working in a fish-scale pattern. Bake the charlotte for about half an hour, until the surface of the bread is golden brown. Remove from the oven and sprinkle caster sugar on top. Serve with fresh custard or thick double cream.

© Rose Prince 2005

Rose Prince

Rose Prince is a freelance food journalist and writer, whose work appears regularly in the *Daily Telegraph*, the *Telegraph Magazine*, *BBC Good Food*, the *Spectator* and the *Tablet*. She has contributed to *The Food Programme*, *Woman's Hour* and *You and Yours* on BBC Radio 4. In 1999 she co-produced *In the Footsteps of Elizabeth David*, a two hour film for Channel 4, presented by Chris Patten. *The New English Kitchen* is her first book. She lives in London with her husband, the journalist Dominic Prince and their two children.

Silvana Franco

Silvana Franco is a food writer and stylist with over a decade of experience working in the food media. She worked as senior writer on *BBC Good Food* and as Food Editor for the *M&S Magazine* before launching into the world of television as a food stylist and writer on *Can't Cook Won't Cook*, *Ainsley's Meals in Minutes*, *Ainsley's Barbecue Bible* and *Ainsley's Gourmet Express*. She now runs her own company, Fork, together with two other food writers, and in 2002 appeared on BBC2 with *The Best*. Her cookery books include *The Student Cookbook* (Merehurst 1994), *Salsas and Ketchups* (Quarto 1995), *Can't Cook, Won't Cook Leaves Home* (BBC Books 1998), *Pizza* (Ryland, Peters and Small 2001), *Pasta* (Ryland, Peters and Small 2002) and *The Best* (BBC Books, 2002).

Lime and Passion Fruit Souffle

Serves 6

400ml carton reduced-fat fresh custard
3 tbsp icing sugar
grated rind of 2 limes
pulp and seeds from 3 ripe passion fruit
3 egg whites
1 tbsp caster sugar

Preheat the oven to 190°C / 375°F/Gas Mark 5 and the grill to medium. Place the custard in a large bowl and stir in the icing sugar, lime rind and passion fruit.

In a separate bowl, whisk the egg whites until stiff. Using a large metal spoon, gently fold the egg whites into the custard. Carefully transfer the mixture to a large soufflé dish, level off the surface and sprinkle with the caster sugar.

Pop the soufflé under a medium grill for 3 minutes until the sugar melts. Transfer to the oven and bake for 20 minutes until well risen and set. Serve swiftly.

Taken from the *Hi Lo Cookbook*

Pat Chapman

Chocolate Custard

Of all the puddings my Raj grandmother made, this was my absolute favourite. Use 'bitter' chocolate, which contains at least 70% cocoa solids. Chocolate Custard is always served hot, and it has the texture of thickish custard. Thinning it down with tinned evaporated milk was one Raj luxury this recipe must have.

Serves 4

140g 'bitter' chocolate (see above)
600ml milk
2 tbsp custard powder
2 tbsp sugar, or more to taste
a few drops of vanilla essence
a pinch or two of salt

Select a heatproof glass bowl which fits comfortably over a saucepan. Cut or break the chocolate into small squares, and put them into the bowl. Bring some water to the simmer in the saucepan. Put the bowl onto the pan, ensuring the bottom does not touch the water. The chocolate will melt fast, helped by stirring.

Using just enough of the milk, (a couple of spoonfuls) make a paste with the custard powder in a large jug.

Bring the milk to the simmer in a 3 litre non-stick saucepan. Little by little, pour it into the jug of custard paste, stirring all the time.

Pour it back into the saucepan, adding the melted chocolate, the sugar, vanilla and the salt.

Stir continuously until it will thicken no further. Serve hot, with a jug of evaporated milk.

Baked Saffron and Cardamom Cream

This is a French crème renversée with a delicate Middle Eastern flavour.

Serves 6

600ml milk
100 – 125g sugar
A good pinch of saffron threads
½ tsp ground cardamom
1 tbsp rose water
4 large eggs

Scald the milk with the sugar, saffron and cardamom and cool to lukewarm. Then add the rosewater.

Beat the eggs and gradually add the milk, beating until well mixed.

Pour into a greased oven dish and bake in a 180°C (350°F Gas Mark 4) oven for about 1 hour and 15 minutes, until the custard has set and the top is lightly browned.

Serve chilled.

Claudia Roden

Photo: Jason Lowe

Claudia Roden was born and brought up in Cairo. She went to school in Paris for three years and to art school in London. Her books have won her many awards. They include *A New Book of Middle Eastern Food* (Penguin UK), *Mediterranean Cookery* (Penguin UK), *The Food of Italy - Region by Region* (Chatto and Windus), *The Book of Jewish Food* (Penguin UK), *Claudia Roden's Invitation to Mediterranean Cookery* (Pavilion and Macmillan), *Tamarind and Saffron* (Penguin UK) and *Picnics and Other Outdoor Feasts* (Grub Street). She presented the BBC TV series *Claudia Roden's Mediterranean Cookery*.

Jamie Oliver

Photo: © David Loftus

Green Tea and Vanilla Panna Cotta with Chocolate Sauce

Serves 4

100ml milk
1 vanilla pod, split and seeds removed
3 green tea bags or 2 heaped tbsp of green tea
350ml double cream
1 ¼ leaves of gelatine, soaked in water
70g icing sugar
30g caster sugar
150ml water
1 level tbsp cocoa powder
100g dark chocolate, broken into pieces

Put the milk, vanilla pod and seeds, tea bags or tea and half the cream in a small pan and slowly simmer for about 10 minutes until reduced by a third. Remove from the heat and extract the tea bags (put the mixture through a sieve if you've used loose tea or your tea bags have burst). Squeeze out the gelatine, discarding the soaking water, then stir the gelatine into the tea mixture and leave to dissolve. Allow to cool a little, then place in the fridge, stirring occasionally until the mixture coats the back of a spoon. Remove the vanilla pod.

Whip together the icing sugar and the remaining cream. Mix the two cream mixtures together. Divide into four metal moulds (small glasses or cappuccino cups also work well). Cover and chill for at least an hour.

Meanwhile, place the caster sugar, the water and the cocoa in a small saucepan and bring to the boil. Take off the heat and stir in the broken chocolate. Stir until dissolved and warm briefly before serving.

To serve, sometimes I dip the mould or cup into some simmering water to loosen the panna cotta, then turn it out on to a plate and spoon the chocolate sauce around it, or – especially if you feel the mixture is a bit wet – you can simply serve the dessert in its cup with chocolate sauce poured over the top.

© Jamie Oliver 2004
www.jamieoliver.com

Photo: © David Loftus 2004

James Martin

Warm Banana Tarte Tatin

This is a very quick and equally delicious tart. Use bananas that have Spotty skins for the best flavour and serve with scoops of a good-quality ice-cream.

Serves 6-8

500g (1lb 2oz) bought puff pastry, thawed if frozen
250g (9oz) caster sugar
25g (1oz) butter, softened
leaves stripped from 1 sprig of fresh rosemary, chopped
8 ripe bananas

Roll out the pastry on a lightly floured surface and cut into a 25cm (10 inch) round. Prick all over with a fork, then leave to rest In the refrigerator while you make the filling.

Place the sugar in a heavy-based saucepan and melt slowly over a very low heat until it turns a mid-caramel colour. You might like to add 1 tbsp of water to help it on its way, but most chefs don't. It is vital not to allow the syrup to bubble even around the edge until all the sugar grains have dissolved; otherwise the mixture will become grainy.

It can help to brush the sides of the pan with a pastry brush dipped in cold water, to prevent any stray sugar grains from causing the syrup to crystallize.

As soon as the sugar turns a mid-caramel colour, plunge the pan base into a sink of cold water to halt the browning. It will spit alarmingly, so make sure that your arm is well covered. Beat in the butter until the mixture turns to a buttery caramel. Pour the caramel into an oven-proof frying pan, or 23cm (9 inch) shallow cake tin, turn and evenly coat the bottom and sides with the caramel.

Heat the oven to 190°C (375°F), Gas Mark 5,

Sprinkle the chopped rosemary over the surface of the caramel, then slice the bananas on top. Finally, place the pastry round over the sliced bananas, pressing the edge down the sides of the filling all the way round.

Bake In the oven for 20-25 minutes until the pastry is crisp and golden. Remove carefully from the oven to prevent spilling the hot caramel. Allow to stand for a few minutes before carefully inverting on to a serving plate. Cut into wedges to serve.

Atul Kochhar

Bhapa Doi-e- Gooler Mishti

(Sweetened steamed yoghurt – with figs in syrup)

The principle behind this dessert is quite like crème caramel. Since India has a huge population of vegetarians, dessert bases are thickened with the reduction method rather than using eggs as thickeners. North Indian Kulfi ice cream has the similar principle. However, in this recipe instead of using 'Rabari' – reduced milk – I have used condensed milk. Figs are called Gooler or Anjeer in India. 'Murrabha', or cooking in syrup technique to preserve, is very old in India, perhaps it came from Persia.

Serves 4 • preparation 10 minutes • cooking 45 minutes

30g Demerara or brown sugar
200g Condensed milk
200g Natural set or Greek yoghurt
10g Pistachio nuts cut into slivers
10g Raisins, soaked in warm water to soften
A pinch of Cardamom powder

In a small pan caramelise the brown sugar and pour it in 4 small ramequin moulds or oven-proof moulds. Whisk together the rest of the ingredients and pour it on the top of the caramel layer. Put these moulds in a baking tray and pour warm water in the tray almost to half the height of the moulds. Bake this pudding in a preheated oven of 150°C for 40 to 50 minutes. Remove and keep aside until required.

(This can be served hot or cold with figs in syrup. This can be served either in the mould or removed from the mould and served on a plate.)

Figs in syrup

4 figs (from late summer)
2 tbsp granulated sugar
1 lemon rind
1 tsp lemon juice
2 cloves
1 inch cinnamon stick
1 star anise

Make a syrup with the sugar, water, lemon juice and rind and spices. Cut each fig into four. Boil the syrup and add figs, simmer for 2 minutes and remove the pan from the heat source. Stand the figs in syrup until it cools. These figs can be used as an accompaniment to various desserts.

Presentation

At Benares, I use blackberry sauce at the base of the plate and accompany this dessert with a blackberry sorbet to balance the sweetness. But using fig syrup can be equally interesting.

Line the plate with the sauce, place "the cake" in the centre of the plate, top it with few pieces of poached figs and sit a neat quenelle or a scoop of sorbet on top and garnish with a mint sprig.

Paul Gayler

Lemon Grass, Coconut and Vanilla Panna Cotta with Passion Fruit-chilli Syrup

Serves 4

1 vanilla pod
2 lemon grass stalks, outer layer removed
350ml (12fl oz) double cream
150ml (¼ pint) unsweetened coconut milk
40g (1½ oz) caster sugar
1½ gelatine leaves
Assortment of exotic fruits (such as mango, papaya, lychee and dragonfruit), peeled and diced, to serve

For the passion fruit-chilli syrup
2 passion fruit, halved
100ml (3½fl oz) stock syrup
Juice and grated zest of ½ a lime
⅛ tsp deseeded and finely diced red chilli

Cut the vanilla pod in half lengthways and scrape out the seeds with the tip of a sharp knife. Bruise the lemon grass and shred it finely. Heat the cream, coconut milk, vanilla seeds, lemon grass and sugar in a pan but do not let it boil.

Meanwhile, cover the gelatine leaves with cold water for 5 minutes, then squeeze out excess water. Remove the cream mixture from the heat, add the softened gelatine and stir until dissolved. Leave to cool, stirring occasionally, then strain into individual tumbler-style glasses and place in the fridge overnight.

For the passion fruit-chilli syrup, scrape the juice and seeds from the passion fruit into a small pan, add the stock syrup and heat gently. Leave for 10-15 minutes to infuse, then strain. Add the lime juice and zest and the diced chilli and leave to cool.

Arrange the exotic fruits on top of the panna cotta, pour over a little of the chilli syrup and serve.

Paul Rankin

Coconut Cream with Marinated Pineapple

Serves 4 – 6
(depending on size of mould)

400ml tin of coconut milk (13–14oz)

4 egg yolks

350g sugar

6 tbsp Malibu liqueur

2 leaves gelatine

240ml whipping cream

½ fresh del Monte pineapple, about 450g before skinning

toasted coconut flakes to garnish

Place the coconut milk in a small pan over a medium heat and bring to the boil. Whisk together the egg yolks and 150g of the sugar until light and fluffy. Add the coconut milk to the egg/sugar mixture whisking continually. Return it to the pan, and keep stirring over a medium heat until the mixture is thick enough to coat the back of a spoon. Remove from the heat.

Soak the gelatine leaves in cold water for 5–10 minutes. Whisk into custard mix until completely dissolved. Add 3 tbsp Malibu to mixture. Strain through a fine sieve to ensure there are no lumpy bits undissolved. Place over a bowl of chilled water to cool.

Or

Warm 3 tbsp of Malibu and sprinkle over 2 tsp powdered gelatine, stirring continuously. Whisk the gelatine mixture into the custard. Strain the custard through a fine sieve and place over a bowl of chilled water to cool.

Whisk the whipping cream to soft peak. When the custard mixture has cooled and thickened to about the same consistency as the cream, gently fold them together until evenly combined. Pour into individual ramekins and place in the fridge to set, preferably overnight.

Peel the pineapple and cut into bite sized pieces. Bring 200ml water and the remaining sugar to the boil. Remove from the heat, and when cool, add the remaining Malibu and the pineapple. Marinate for no more than 2 hours, or the pineapple will lose its freshness.

To serve, turn out the creams on to chilled serving plates and place the pineapple pieces around and on top of them. Decorate with coconut flakes and a couple of small pineapple leaves.

Genevieve McGough

Lime Marinated Paw Paw and Lychees with Coconut sorbet

Serves 4

Coconut sorbet
400ml / 14fl oz of coconut cream
400ml / 14fl oz milk
180g/6oz caster sugar
60g/2oz glucose syrup

Bring the above ingredients to a simmer in a medium sized pot stirring occasionally.

Remove from the heat and cool to room temperature.

Refrigerate for 2 hours then churn in a gelato machine.

Make sure the sorbet has an hour to set in the freezer after churning so it is firm enough for serving.

Lime marinated paw paw and lychees
1 paw paw
500g/1lb tin of lychees in syrup
1 fresh lime grated zest and juice
1 lime cut into wedges

Skin the paw paw, slice in half and scoop out the seeds with a spoon.

Dice the paw paw into large chunks and place in a mixing bowl.

Drain the lychees and add them to the mixing bowl along with half a cup of the syrup from the can.

Add the lime zest and juice.

Stir a little to incorporate, then chill until serving time.

To serve, spoon the fruit salad into bowls and top with a scoop of coconut sorbet and wedges of fresh lime.

Enid Humfrey

Earl Grey Sorbet

570ml water
170g sugar
Thinly pared rind and juice of 2 lemons
2 tbsp Earl Grey tea leaves
1 egg white

Put water, sugar, lemon juice and rind in saucepan. Bring to boil and simmer for 5 minutes.

Add the tea leaves. Cool the mixture and then strain

Freeze the mixture until it is half-solid

Whisk the egg white until just stiff and fold it into the frozen mixture

Freeze again until frozen

Green Tea Ice Cream

This is a very simple recipe given me by a Japanese friend, I have used it several times

750g vanilla ice cream – either home-made or good quality commercial ice cream, softened
150ml whipping cream
2 tbsp matcha green tea powder dissolved in 100ml hot water

Mix together the ice cream and whipped cream in a bowl

Blend the green tea mixture into the ice cream to create a green ice cream or swirl it through to create a marbled effect.

Freeze, preferably in an ice cream maker

Spiced Vanilla Ice Cream

(makes a good two pint tub)

- 8 cups of double cream
- 8 cups of whole milk
- 4 cups of caster sugar
- Zest of 2 oranges
- Zest of 1 lemon
- 2 cinnamon sticks
- 4 crushed cloves
- 4-6 whole allspice
- 3-4 whole star anise
- 1 whole nutmeg cut in half
- 3-4 cardamon pods
- 1 tsp ground ginger
- 1 tsp ground mixed spice
- 2 vanilla pods
- 20 egg yolks
- 4 tbsp port

Place the cream, milk, spices and fruit zest in a plastic container and leave in the fridge for around 16 hours then transfer to a saucepan and heat until simmering.

Put the egg yolks in a large bowl and strain the liquid over the yolks and caster sugar, being sure to whisk as you pour the liquid or the yolks may scramble in the heat.

Pour the strained egg and liquid back into the pan and return to a gentle heat. Stir constantly for around 5 minutes or until the mixture coats the back of your wooden spoon (to test, lift the spoon from the pan and run your finger across the back of it, the custard should hold and not run across the gap your finger has just made).

Strain the mixture once more into a clean plastic container and place this into a larger bowl and surround with ice to ensure the liquid cools quickly and ceases cooking.

Once cold, add the port and churn in an ice cream machine according to the manufacturer's instructions.

© Justin Piers Gellatly, St. John's head baker and pastry chef.

Justin Piers Gellatly

Photo: John Deehan

Justin Piers Gellatly began working at the original St. John in Smithfield in April 2000 as chef de partie in Fergus Henderson's kitchen. Having moved in to St. John's in-house bakery soon after as pastry chef and excelling in his new role, Justin was a natural to head up the new bakery and pastry section in St. John Bread and Wine which opened in Commercial Street near Spitalfields market in May 2003. Justin's role at Bread and Wine is pivotal, as he not only developed the recipes for the desserts enjoyed by dining room customers but also was fundamental in creating the formulas for the sour doughs and other loaves baked every morning at St. John Bread and Wine. He is married to Louise, also a chef, and lives in South London.

Ed Baines

Goat's Cheese & Pear Crostata with Chilli Lime Syrup

Serves 4 - 6

Fruit served with cheese at the end of a meal is a culinary tradition, the two complementing each other so well. This recipe combines the flavours of the fruit and cheese, and is a wonderful alternative to cheesecake.

400g (14oz) puff pastry
2 cooking apples
2 pears
juice of 1 lime
225g (8oz) goat's cheese log
1 egg
a splash of milk

for the chilli lime syrup
1 red chilli, deseeded and chopped
1 tbsp sugar
juice of 1 lime
2 tbsp olive oil
salt and pepper

Preheat the oven to 180°C/350°F/Gas Mark 4. Roll out the puff pastry to a rectangle slightly larger than a sheet of A4 paper. Place it on a chopping board and put it in the fridge to allow it to rest before cooking.

Peel the apples and pears and core them, then cut them into thin slices. Place the sliced fruit in a large bowl and pour over the juice of one of the limes. Using a hot wet knife, cut the goat's cheese in half lengthwise, and slice these across into the thinnest half moons of cheese you can manage.

Remove the pastry from the fridge. In a small bowl, whisk the egg with a touch of milk and brush this glaze around the edges of the pastry, about 1cm (½ inch) in all the way round. Now place a slice of apple followed by one of pear across the pastry in lines ensuring you leave the same gap of clear pastry around the edge. Arrange the goat's cheese slices to overlap between the lines of fruit as evenly as you can. I'm suggesting you do it this way as I often find that there are always many more slices of fruit than goat's cheese, unless you've sliced it incredibly thinly.

Place the crostata in the oven and cook for 15-20 minutes, until crisp around the edges and the fruit is golden brown – the cheese should have slightly melted and have a dark-brown crispy surface. Remove from oven and allow to rest for 5 minutes.

Whilst the crostata is cooking and resting, make the chilli lime syrup: using a pestle and mortar, grind the chilli to a paste with the sugar. Add the lime juice, followed by the olive oil, a small pinch of salt and a twist of black pepper. Mix together well. If you don't have a pestle and mortar, use the back of a spoon in a bowl. Gently drizzle this over the crostata.

Taken from *Entertain* by Ed Baines. Published by Kyle Cathie 2001

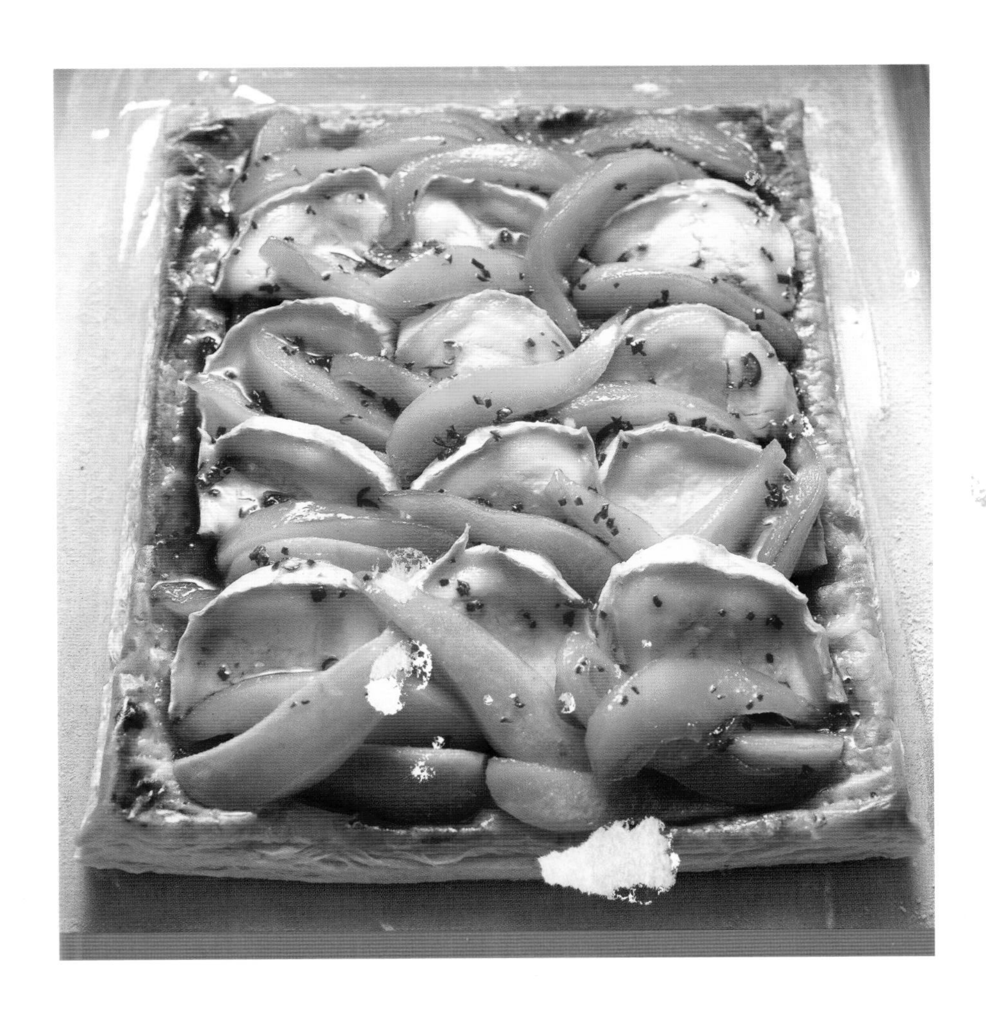

Index